Storm Chaser

In pursuit of untamed skies

STORM CHASER

In pursuit of untamed skies

BY WARREN FAIDLEY

THE WEATHER CHANNEL
Atlanta, Georgia

Published for The Weather Channel
by B.V.E. Products, Inc.
2600 Cumberland Parkway
Atlanta, Georgia 30339

ISBN 1-888763-00-0

Book design by Regina Dalton-Fischel
Front cover design and illustrations by Lisa Ammerman
Editorial Team: Eileen Lichtenfeld, Wendy Stahl, Stu Ostro,
Dennis Smith, Ardel Banas, Phoebe Snow, and Keith Westerlage

Manufactured in the United States of America
Printed by Image Graphics, Inc., Paducah, KY
Library of Congress Catalog Card Number: 96-83284

FOREWORD

It has been said that some people are weatherwise, but most are otherwise. Warren Faidley is decidedly weatherwise.

The Weather Channel has known Warren Faidley for a number of years. We have a great deal of respect for his work and have featured it in our documentaries and publications. Warren's photography is world-renowned and the result of considerable knowledge, talent and effort. He is also held in high esteem as a storm chaser and served as a technical consultant to the movie *Twister.*

I first came to know Warren through his stunning photographs of lightning. His lightning photography has great meaning to me, as my personal fascination with weather was initiated by a phobia of lightning. Warren's early work primarily depicts lightning in Arizona. Over the years he has added the Great Plains and their stormy phenomena to his repertoire. Severe thunderstorms and tornadoes develop elsewhere in the country and the world, but the Great Plains of the United States represent a unique natural laboratory. Here a potent combination of atmospheric ingredients often comes together to create spectacular storms.

Helped along by the lack of mountainous obstructions, warm and moist air from over the Gulf of Mexico surges toward the north and northwest, clashing with cool air moving down from Canada. Dry air pushes east from the western mountains and deserts. Throw in energetic winds aloft and the result can be "supercells," which are intense, rotating thunderstorms—and the target of storm chasers in the Plains.

Chasing is fun but requires hard work. To be successful, the storm chaser must make a precise and accurate weather forecast, have intimate knowledge of severe storm structure, and keep an eye on the sky while navigating a road network that may be less than ideal. The real essence of the chase, though, is the adrenaline rush of coming face-to-face with the forces of nature. This is the ultimate weatherwise thrill, as I can attest to from my own limited experience with chasing. The reasons why people chase may vary, but being in awe of the power of weather is a common thread.

Storm chasing is also dangerous, and Warren Faidley is not careless. His chases are well-organized, professional expeditions, involving meticulous planning and specialized equipment. In *Storm Chaser,* he takes us into his world of stalking lightning in the desert, tornadoes in the Plains, and hurricanes along the coast. Along with his beautiful photos he gives us a good primer on chasing terminology, and a sound explanation of the meteorology associated with tornadoes and other forms of severe weather.

I pursue my passion for weather predominately through my role at The Weather Channel. So, unlike Warren, chasing for me is not a full-time job. But in this book I get an opportunity to live vicariously through him. If you are one of us, you will too. If otherwise, you will get a glimpse of what makes us weatherwise.

Stu Ostro
Senior Meteorologist
The Weather Channel

front cover: Tornado, NE of Pampa, Texas. May 29, 1994

below: A lightning display from a July storm over Tucson

INTRODUCTION

The weather is my sustenance. It is my professional life and my social life and everything in between. It is fickle and indecisive, and it keeps me from doing a million other things. But I neither seek, nor want, anything different.

I chase tornadoes, lightning, hurricanes and other vicious elements. To the best of my knowledge, I am the only person, worldwide, whose livelihood depends entirely on filming and taking pictures of the weather.

My line of work is a fusion of art, science, intuition and luck. I chase storms with cameras, computers and technology. I improvise where needed to learn about storms in other ways. For example, the nose. Stockyard manure smells different (worse) when it's going to rain, a clerk in Lubbock once explained. "When it stinks in the spring, we have thunderstorms."

My life is unpredictable. One moment, I'm casually reading a weather map. Seconds later, I'm running after clouds. This inconsistant lifestyle has a price. I've drunk coffee that spans the consumable pH scale, and I've lost count of the number of times I prayed after eating in roadside cafes. Storm chasing has been hell on relationships. And how many people, in how many towns, in how many accents, have gazed at me like I have five heads and asked, "You do *what* for a living?"

Let me offer this explanation: life as a storm chaser/photographer is no different from other journalism careers. Instead of specializing in the coverage of war, sports, or fashion, I have made a successful living and a unique career out of forecasting, intercepting, and photographing both the beautiful and the grotesque of the atmosphere.

I have ventured across thousands of majestic and desolate miles linked by familiar and unknown paths, populated with intriguing characters. My journeys are filled with breathtaking colors and rare shapes, each one unique, existing for only a few precious moments—but captured forever on film. Chasing tempts me with irresistible enigmas—never knowing what the new day will bring.

The quest for storms has rewarded me with moments of victory and awe. It has also made me shake with fear. It has left me standing at the doorstep of disaster, humbled by the cold and violent reality of the *nature* of my pursuit of nature.

Warren Faidley
Tucson, Arizona, July 9, 1995

Adrenaline-Fixed in Kansas

Chase Log: June 15, 1992. North-central Kansas.

The new storm had potential to kill. I had intercepted two tornadoes earlier in the day, including a ghostly gray vortex which churned through the outskirts of Plainville, Kansas, spewing a fountain of debris as I drove alongside.

Now the heavenly white clouds of the afternoon's second severe storm exploded into the baby blue sky, looking more like the cloud from an atomic bomb blast than a supercell, the most powerful of all land mass thunderstorms and a prolific producer of violent tornadoes. I was in my element and savoring every moment.

I headed north on Highway 281, towards Osborne, as the storm grew stronger and closer by the second.

previous pages: A small tornado develops under a spectacular wall cloud northeast of Miami, Texas. May 29, 1994.

right: Storm clouds close in.

Conditions were ripe for the creation of rotating supercells. The clouds around the base of this storm appeared to be organizing for a tornado.

As I descended into a valley sprinkled with farms, I reached over and pushed the search button on the radio of the rental car, desperate for a weather update. "Come on, damn it. This is already a severe storm," I mumbled. "Somebody has got to be watching." I knew that selected radio stations in this part of the country take the weather seriously and usually broadcast continuous coverage, even live reports from observers in vehicles. Information is critical to personal safety. Even the smallest tidbit of data has importance to my photography—to say nothing of my life itself.

The radio locked onto a news report which said the Plainview tornado had not killed anyone. I was surprised, in light of all the debris I had seen falling from the sky.

Between the news and a commercial for hail insurance, the station offered a radar update. The message was foreboding. The new storm was "becoming increasingly severe," it said, and warned residents of Osborne county to prepare for tornadoes and large hail. I grabbed the hand-held radio scanner that receives the National Weather Service broadcasts, and activated all of the north-central Kansas frequencies. Nothing but static. I was out of range.

North of the valley, the highway rose over a small knoll. This vantage point allowed me to view the entire structure of the storm. I pulled to the side of the road, reached for my 35mm camera, got out and dashed to the crest of the hill, which was lined with a barbed-wire fence. "Keep your distance from a fence." I remembered the chaser's rule and backed away slightly. A lightning strike to that fence, even miles away, would convert it to a power line and finish off any unsuspecting soul.

Away from the fence, I craned my neck toward the spectacle. The storm sprawled over the landscape some twenty miles, a large surface for a single storm, even in storm-worn Kansas. This storm was now a perfectly sculpted supercell. The main body was a mass of snow-white clouds, some appearing as cauliflower-shaped heaps, so dense they appeared rock hard. Halfway up the side of the storm, at

thirty thousand feet, a pair of thin "Saturn rings" circled the body, indicating storm rotation. At the top of the towering cloud mass, a huge, anvil-shaped cloud spread outward in a circular pattern, its thick edges lined with knuckle-like features. Protruding over the top of the anvil was a dome-like cloud, pushed upward by an intense updraft.

What astonished me most was that I could actually see the entire storm expanding—like lungs filling with moist air, reaching a pinnacle almost twice the height of Mount Everest.

I scanned the lower levels of the storm, near the ground. To the northeast, I could see the dark downdraft area, where heavy rain and hail were falling from great heights. To the south side of the rain shafts, bright white streaks denoted sheets of large hail, glistening in the sun. A few miles to the north, bowing across the entire leading edge of the storm, was a gust front—a harmless, yet foreboding, grayish-green cloud caused by the condensation of falling rain and ice. This was the frightening sight the people in Osborne would see just before the storm hit.

I was mainly interested in the southwestern base, at the back of the storm. Within this region of updraft and downdraft interactions, most tornadoes begin their descent. Within minutes of my arrival, a blackish-blue, circular cloud mass began to lower from the center of the updraft base. Less than five hundred feet off the ground, the lowering, or "wall cloud," was at least a half-mile in diameter. Soon, rows of ragged appendages formed on the outside edges of the wall cloud, resembling the rusty jaws of a gigantic bear trap.

I watched as the wall cloud harmlessly hovered a few miles away. I knew that less than fifty percent of all wall clouds produce tornadoes. I had played this game of cat-and-mouse before, and I wasn't too concerned—that is, until I noticed the wall cloud had begun to rotate like an enormous carousel. And instead of the storm's initial northeastern track, it was moving eastward, toward me.

The smell of freshly cut fields gave way to an onrush of invigorating cold air. The storm was exhaling and something was about to happen.

I had been out of the car for what seemed like brief minutes. But my curiosity had led to the supreme mistake of chasers—losing track of position. The supercell was turning and making a beeline for my hillside perch. I made a dash for the car as a rogue bolt of lightning whizzed overhead. I watched the reflection in the car's windshield. The ensuing thunderclap was the storm's way of laughing at me.

I swung open the door, cursed, dropped a roll of film on

left: A supercell storm with a rounded anvil cloud near Plainville, Kansas

right: An impressive, rotating wall cloud, precursor to a possible tornado, hovers over the northern Kansas landscape.

the ground, cursed again, picked it up and blew the dirt off. I climbed back in the car, placed the camera on the passenger-side floorboard, released the hand brake, looked ahead, then over my left shoulder, put the car in drive and slammed on the gas. (I always leave the car running—just in case.)

The car spun around as the squealing tires filled the air with rocks, dust and white smoke. I fishtailed onto the pavement, heading south, back toward the valley.

In my rearview mirror, the agitated clouds began to overtake the hill like an avalanche. For a moment, I felt I had outwitted yet another storm. But this had been too easy.

All at once, a gust of wind rammed the car. I grabbed the steering wheel with both hands to avoid being pushed off the road. After I regained control, I reached back to the passenger seat and grabbed the video camera. I turned it on and, while steering with one hand, pointed it toward the rear window. The sun was fading, and I was left with the all-too-familiar feeling of being in jeopardy.

A second series of gusts buffeted the car, first from the left, then from the right. I let the camera fall to the passenger seat and returned my hands to the steering wheel. Seconds later, I slammed on the brakes as a piece of fractured plywood cartwheeled across the highway and toward the storm. I stretched my neck out the window to see what was above me, not daring to stop. Overhead and to the right, I could see the bear trap's teeth. "Damn!" I yelled out, as I pressed the accelerator to the floor, recalling the earlier tornadoes and feeling stupid for having fallen into this crisis.

The car's engine raced, but the car itself was another story. It felt heavy and sluggish against the wind. It reminded me of a childhood dream: a giant is pursuing me, and I can't outrun him no matter how hard I try.

Then, something amazing occurred. Winds began to circulate through the car's open windows. Every piece of loose paper began to float as if suspended in zero gravity. The pages in my atlas and diary turned one by one, as if an invisible hand was thumbing through them. For a fleeting moment, I was entertained, but my thoughts turned to horror as I realized I was directly under a forming tornado.

I frantically scanned the sides of the road, looking for a place to abandon the car and a ditch to lie in. With only a mile to go before cloud-free skies, I made my decision. At full speed I pressed on, not daring to waste precious seconds looking for uncertain shelter. Even so, I expected the car to be lifted away at any moment, as I tried to keep the floating paper from blocking my view.

Suddenly, as the car was about to pass under the last dark cloud, my ears popped. A fierce gust of wind rocked the car and whisked the suspended papers out the windows. A deep rumbling of thunder echoed. Bright sunshine filled the car.

Sunshine! Glorious sunshine. I had, at last, escaped the storm's grip.

I drove another mile or so before pulling over to take another look. My hands were drenched with sweat. Behind me lay a long trail of broken tree branches. The storm was still rotating angrily as it moved across the Kansas landscape. Later that afternoon, it would produce several tornadoes.

After the clouds passed, I returned to the site where the storm had gobbled up my papers. I scoured the countryside but discovered not even a scrap.

It was time to move on to the next storm.

A truck attempts to outrun the advancing maelstrom.

From Topeka to Tucson

Chase Log: The Beginning.

Beware May 11.

Of all the days each year when a tornado might touch down, this is one of the most dangerous.

On May 11, 1953 a tornado swept through Waco, Texas, killing 114 people. On that day in 1970, two fast-moving twisters hit Lubbock, Texas, killing 26 and destroying nearly a quarter of the town.

May 11 is not only one of the busiest and most treacherous days for me as a storm chaser, it is also the day in 1957, in Topeka, Kansas, that I was born. Nowadays, if I'm lucky, my birthday is toasted over a can of beer and a chocolate cupcake in Dumas, Texas, or Dodge City, Kansas. It is not a gala event.

This image was shot as a two-minute time exposure from a hill near Tucson.

Less than one year after my birth, in the heart of "Tornado Alley," my father, a civil service computer programmer, was transferred to Mobile, Alabama. This move was, in a way, my first escape from a tornado. In 1966, a massive tornado swept through Topeka, killing 17 people.

I recall my earliest fascination with storms while growing up in Mobile. Not only was Mobile home to tropical weather, but the passage of spring and fall frontal systems triggered severe storms and tornadoes. I remember huddling with my mother, sister, and baby brother in the hallway of our home after a storm warning. On at least one occasion, I tried to sneak out to take a look, only to be grabbed by my mom, who scolded me with a pointed finger. "You want to be picked up by a twister?" she asked.

No doubt, my interests in tornadoes were awakened by the film version of *The Wizard of Oz*. The film was broadcast once a year, and, without fail, I was seated in front of the television, awaiting my favorite part, the tornado. As a child, I imagined a brave "storm chaser" had risked his life filming a real one. It was only years later that I realized the Oz vortex was a special effect created by the geniuses at MGM.

My first hands-on confrontation with severe weather occurred when I was nine during a boat outing on Mobile Bay. While my father and I were exploring an old harbor filled with dilapidated cargo ships, a squall, harmlessly poised in the distance, headed our way. My father raced the 6-horsepower engine of our 11-foot aluminum boat in an attempt to outrun the storm. I sat at the bow, holding on tightly, bouncing up and down over the white caps. "Are we going to make it?" I asked as the boat filled with water. My dad nodded an unsure "Yes." Just as the leading edge of the boiling black clouds reached our boat, we made it to shore and the shelter of a small concrete building. To this day, I vividly recall the dark clouds

above: Warren Faidley at age two. Mobile, Alabama.

right: A cumulonimbus cloud rockets into the Tucson sky.

and even the thick, salty smell of the storm. Years later, my father confessed he thought we wouldn't make it.

My curiosity got the best of me when a neighbor's house was hit by lightning. I ran down the street following the fire engine, and when I reached the front yard, I saw a huge, shirtless man standing at the door, rubbing his beet-red potbelly. Sipping from a beer can, he told the people gathered around the house that he was watching the *I Love Lucy* show when a lightning bolt hit the roof antenna. The charge went into the house and blew up his television set. Lightning leaped from the television and hit him in the stomach, he said, singeing his skin. He quickly became the celebrity of our neighborhood. For days, kids knocked on his door and asked to see his belly and the charred television set in the back yard. He enjoyed the attention and conducted detailed tours, holding another beer can.

In October of 1966 my father was transferred to Tucson, Arizona. I had already lived in both the nation's tornado and hurricane alleys. Now, I would reside in one of the world's lightning hot spots. I became especially interested to see what everyone called "the monsoons." My wait wasn't long.

My first monsoon encounter came in July 1967. I watched billowing white clouds rocket into the afternoon sky, pushed upward by surface temperatures of well over 110 degrees Fahrenheit and a supply of moist air from Mexico. The clouds eventually merged and filled the southern horizon as a single massive thunderhead, with a dark and foreboding base.

The thunderstorms developed daily in July and August. They blanketed the city with a dust cloud, then pounded it with wind, flooding rain and spectacular lightning. At night, I lay in my top bunk watching the lightning bolts dance outside the window and listened to the sound of thunder. The acrid smell of wet creosote bushes seeped in through the half-opened window.

By the age of 12, I was ready to experience the monsoon firsthand.

After the year's first heavy monsoon rainstorm, the runoff filled a usually dry lake bed near our home. A roaring wall of muddy, earthy-smelling water would come sweeping down a narrow arroyo toward the lake. Once the first big storm hit and the water began to flow, a red alert—the type only kids can hear—was sounded. We raced our bikes along the wash and escorted the torrent as it approached the lake bed. It was an amusing, but hazardous, place to play.

While I was walking with a group along the sides of the freshly flooded lake, a portion of the bank collapsed, sending a girl and me tumbling into turbulent waters. I bobbed up and down in the water, holding my breath until my lungs were crying for air. I will never forget the feeling. As I went under the water, gasping what I thought would be my last breath and taking in a mouth full of muddy water, I literally saw my life flash before me. This was death, I was certain. But just as I felt I would pass out, we were carried by the current to a shallow patch where we

A rare photograph of damaging downburst winds from a monsoon storm over southwest Tucson

could stand and lift our heads from the water. From then on I found drier, less deadly things to chase—at least for a while.

My next adventure involved dust devils, or just "devils" as we called them. Dust devils are vortices of swirling air caused by thermals rising from the hot desert floor. The rotating air takes on the classic funnel shape as dust and debris fill the vortex, mimicking the appearance of a small tornado. In the Southwest, it is not uncommon to see dust devils frequently when the temperatures climb to 100 degrees and more.

Impressive dust devils appeared in the dusty vacant lots surrounding my neighborhood. While watching one of these vortices from the seat of my bicycle, I developed my first chase plan. It was not complicated. I decided to ride my bike into the center of the funnel and see what was inside. Racing back to the neighborhood, I gathered my usual band of explorers—save for a couple whose mothers worried about "that Faidley kid" and his wacky adventures.

We donned jackets and safety goggles and rode in formation to the lot, where we made several unsuccessful attempts at entering a dust devil. One unfortunate test pilot among us discovered that the opening of a mouth in a dust cloud was a poor maneuver. Another pal cut short his valiant attempt when a giant tumbleweed flew out of the dust cloud and hit him in the back, sending a load of spiny stickers into his shirt.

My opportunity came as a particularly large devil developed in the center of the lot. I gathered speed, summoned my courage, put on my goggles and took aim. I held my breath and pedaled straight toward the devil. As I broke through the swirling wall of the vortex, I fell off my bike, startled to discover that there was no wind resistance inside the funnel. I was in a large,

A dust devil forms over a vacant lot near Tucson.

hollow cylinder. The interior of the devil was still and virtually dust-free, illuminated by a weird orange hue, caused, I suppose, by sun filtering through the spinning wall of fine desert grit. Tumble weeds, newspapers and other debris were imbedded in the circulation.

Above, I could see the upper regions of the vortex as it oscillated in a snake-like fashion, eventually expanding into a deep blue sky. A constant thrashing noise was all I could hear. The temperature outside the dust devil was about 100 degrees, but it was much hotter inside, and difficult to breathe. For a minute, I was able to ride within the fifteen-yard circumference of the dust devil. But the show abruptly ended when one of the walls crashed into me. I was thrown clear of the funnel, which disintegrated into wispy strands of slowly falling dust. I was greeted by fellow chasers who, having lost sight of me, feared that I had been lifted away. I was elated. My chase had been a success.

False Starts and a Camera.

Shortly after I graduated from high school, I left home to pursue a career as a Navy fighter pilot. During the evening hours, I attended college part-time, and during the day I worked. By 1978 I had only been able to put myself through two years of college. I was broke, depressed and unable to continue school. I shelved my flight plans, and for the next two years, I lived in poverty, scrounging for meals and working odd jobs.

I decided to make one last attempt at my flight plans. I sold the few valuables that I had owned at a swap meet, got a government loan and enrolled at the University of Arizona. Everything was going fine until I took the military pilot medical exam. I failed. My eyesight, which had once

Flood waters devour a building in Tucson. October 1983.

been 20/10 had diminished to 20/40. The military required a minimum of 20/20. I was devastated.

On a whim, I raced stock cars for a year. The sponsor's money dried up, so I returned to work and school. The driving experience would, however, save my life in later endeavors.

I reached senior status in 1982, with no solid major other than pre-law studies. I could never endure sitting in a law office or a courtroom all day, so I walked into a counselor's office and asked, "What's the quickest, cheapest and easiest way to get out of this place?" He looked over my credits. A journalism degree would have me out of school in less than two semesters, he said. "Sign me up," I responded.

My journalism classes included an optional photo course. I immersed myself in news photography. I slept at night with a radio scanner turned on and developed the talent of snoozing while listening to the scanner. If a big fire or other newsworthy event occurred, I would automatically wake up, grab my camera bag and beat everyone to the scene. I sold my images to local newspapers and the wire services.

In October 1983, I covered my first major weather-related story, when the southwestern U.S. was racked by flooding. As a freelancer, I spent the two days, and most of the nights, shooting every flood image I could. The wire services sent my images to publications around the world. My earnings: a whopping $50 for two days of work. It was also during the floods that I met an aggressive photojournalist named Tom Willett.

In the fall of 1984, I was chosen as one of the recipients of the William Randolph Hearst Foundation Journalism award. Shortly thereafter, I was offered a full-time position as a photographer with the local newspaper where Tom was employed.

Newspaper work was the best possible training ground for a future storm chaser. I could shoot all the color film I wanted and see the results almost immediately. I learned how to shoot quickly and produce effective images under deadline. I spent day and night chasing news stories. Tom and I often competed with each other to see who could get to the scene the fastest and get the best photograph. There were a handful of occasions when we barely escaped with our jobs, let alone our lives.

After a few years, the novelty of photojournalism wore off. The monotony and office politics of a small newspaper took their toll.

I began to look for a way out.

above: One of Warren Faidley's first lightning photographs. A double-exposure shot from his apartment balcony. Tucson, 1983.

right: Storm clouds at sunset over Tucson. July 1985.

The Great Escape

I don't remember the moment I decided to put lightning on film, but my earliest efforts were conducted during my college photojournalism studies in 1982. My childhood fascination with storms and my new-found photography interests were a natural fusion. And the pursuit of something as powerful, elusive and risky as a lightning bolt was something I could not resist.

My first attempts to photograph lightning were feeble at best, limited to a roll of black and white film shot from the balcony of my apartment with a single lens camera that I borrowed from the school. There were few exposure guidelines in existence, yet I had the fortune of finding a newspaper article about Tom Ives, one of the first professional photographers to shoot lightning—and make money from it. The article contained the guidelines for photographing lightning. Moreover, the story was inspiring—my new pursuits had economic possibilities. Our first face-to-face meeting, several years later, took place, appropriately, at the top of a Tucson hill as we both pursued shots of the same storm.

My first color images of lightning were taken in 1985 while working at the newspaper. And as the boredom with my job at the paper mounted, I spent more time running to hilltops during the summer monsoon, casually shooting lightning storms between evening assignments. I began to spend my spare time in the science library at the University of Arizona, pouring over literature and films about lightning and severe weather. Learning everything I could about storms would hopefully translate into better images. During the course of my self-education, I discovered that I lived within a day's drive of the western fringe of an intriguing place nicknamed "Tornado Alley."

I chose to stick it out at the newspaper for one more year, save money, then quit and work as a freelance photographer. I would also devote more time to chasing storms as a way to mix travel with adventure and photography.

In late spring of 1987, I decided to escape to Tornado Alley.

right: Lightning near Marana, Arizona

Tornado Alley

Chase Log: May 22, 1987.
Saragosa, Texas.

We sensed something was terribly wrong, even in the dark, as we approached. Our headlights illuminated remains of splintered power poles that looked as though they had been hit with a giant sledgehammer. Beyond our headlights, small pockets of bright lights, powered by loud generators, dotted the landscape where the town used to be. A barrage of red, blue, and yellow flashing emergency lights cast a carnival-like glow into the hazy air.

My first tornado chase had turned into a baptism of fire.

It had started with my decision at noon on May 22, 1987, to head to New Mexico and hunt for tornadoes. A morning forecast for

Clouds gather at sunset near Amarillo, Texas during a June thunderstorm.

eastern New Mexico and west Texas on the television was enough to persuade me that now was the time. I called Tom Willett.

Tom had become an accomplished lightning photographer himself, with similar interests of venturing into the Alley. He also possessed two important virtues of chasing: patience and knowing when to back off. To our benefit, his photo stock house in New York needed graphic storm pictures. Thus, we forged a chase partnership.

Tom has a splendid sense of humor; what makes him a great friend is that he endures mine. Once, when he thought he was the target of a practical joke, he recommended to a mystery caller that Warren Faidley should be contacted for a supposed "assistant photographer" position for a *Playboy* Magazine centerfold shoot near Tucson. The call turned out to be legitimate. I got the job.

Armed with a camera bag, extra clothing, gas station road maps, an amateur knowledge of tornado forecasting and a few years of monsoon storm experience, we hit the road in a rental car. We headed east along I-10 on our debut tornado chase.

We were anxious and excited, discussing our visions of incredible storms and tornadoes like a couple of schoolboys. We thought we were experts. Not once did we consider that this premier chase would teach us a humbling lesson about our new pursuits.

My plan was simple. After leaving Tucson around 2 p.m., we would head towards New Mexico. From Las Cruces, we would continue east on US 70 towards Alamogordo, turn south on I-10 to El Paso or go north along I-25 in the direction of Albuquerque.

Tom Willett with an exploding cloud mass behind him

Our destination would be determined by storms we could see in the distance. My only miscalculation was leaving Tucson so late. I tried to console myself by telling Tom, "No problem, we can be in central New Mexico by sunset, get some great lightning, and be ready for some tornadoes tomorrow." Looking into the rearview mirror, I saw the setting sun and knew that any storm within our reach would have to be pursued in total darkness.

As we approached Las Cruces at dusk, our attention was drawn by what appeared to be a line of thunderstorm tops about 70 miles east, in the direction of El Paso. From Las Cruces we continued east on I-10, with our view hampered by the Organ Mountains, north of El Paso. But as we turned the big curve along the Rio Grande, with Mexico to our right, our view expanded, and we could clearly see a tremendous line of storms cranking away to the east, filled with constant internal flashes of lightning. "Damn, now that's a storm!" said Tom.

It was in the eastern fringes of El Paso, as I tried to find a 9 p.m. news update, that we heard this ominous message: "This is AP radio news. Authorities report that as many as 30 people may have been killed earlier this evening when a tornado struck the small community of Saragosa, Texas, southwest of Midland. Details are sketchy at this hour, but rescuers are reported to be continuing their search for victims."

Tom and I glanced at each other. I had an expressionless opened mouth. Then our journalistic instincts kicked in. "Quick, grab the map!" I told Tom. "Find Saragosa. We've got to be close." Tom looked over the map, checked the index, but could not find any town called "Saragosa." "Check it with a Z, for Zaragoza," I said. "Not here," he responded. I took the next exit and pulled into a gas station. Tom ran inside and asked the clerk, while I scoured the map. Then I found a small dot with "Saragosa" printed next to it, about 192 miles east of El Paso, or a little over two and a half hours away if we pushed it. I sounded the horn and Tom ran back to the car. "I've found it! It's just down the road!" We were about to assume the role of journalists in addition to our chaser identities.

The only obstacle between us and west Texas was the storm we had been approaching. About 30 miles from El Paso, we hit its western edge. The lightning alone was spectacular. Constant flashes throughout the cloud masses were complemented by bolts leaping from cloud to cloud and from cloud to ground. As we penetrated the storm, I felt it close in, smothering us with heavy rain, small hail and a constant, thunderous pounding from the lightning discharges. It felt as though the universe was unattended for a moment and some maniac was in charge. It was unlike anything I had encountered in Arizona.

With the monsoon thunder-boomers, my biggest fear was lightning. Now, new menaces were surfacing—namely tornadoes and large hail. And since my first-hand knowledge of these dangers was limited, they instantly became frightening. "I sure the hell hope this storm's not the same one that hit Saragosa," I said. We both glanced nervously out the windows and watched the lightning illuminate ominous clouds.

Approaching a lightning storm near El Paso, Texas

Sixty miles west of Saragosa the storm diminished and was trailed by a thick fog bank. The fog was occasionally tinted with the red glow of emergency vehicles that passed us, en route to Saragosa. We took Exit 206 off I-10 and tried to enter Saragosa from the south, but a volunteer deputy, standing at a road block with a coffee cup in his hand, would not let us pass.

"Can't let anybody through. It's pretty bad down there," he said. I displayed a handful of official press passes. "Yes, sir, I understand, but we're journalists and we need access," I said. "Not tonight," he barked, and I deduced that his patience should not be tried any further.

We had been through similar problems with access before, and I figured other journalists would already be there. "OK, thanks for your help. We'll wait 'til morning," I said. We headed back west along the frontage road. It was time to resort to Plan B: swing around and enter the town from the north.

A mile down the dark frontage road, Tom shouted, "Hey, look out!" In the middle of the road was a large uprooted cottonwood tree. This was the first sign a tornado had passed through. "I wonder how many people driving on I-10 just missed being nailed by the tornado when it crossed," I asked. We maneuvered around the tree and circled to the north.

We were now in the midst of the multi-colored emergency lights. We parked at the edge of town, assembled our equipment and walked along the debris and mud-laden road toward the lights. The smell of destruction—freshly splintered wood mixed with the odors of gas generators and wet fabric—filled the air. Several hundred feet away, two Texas State Department of Public Safety (DPS) officers got out of a patrol car. In unison, they put their hats on. "Here we go again," I whispered to Tom.

"May we help you?" one said.

"Yes, sir," I responded, "We're journalists from Arizona on assignment in Texas and just happened to hear about the tornado. ..."

Just then my conversation was cut short as a pair of headlights pierced the misty air and landed on us.

The officers stared at the vehicle, a small school bus, as it approached. One of them said somberly, "That's the morgue bus."

We stood silently as the bus passed into the mist.

The officers looked at our credentials and advised us of the usual hazards associated with a disaster, including exposed nails and collapsing debris. We thanked them and moved on.

We came upon the flattened remains of a home that resembled a pile of scrap lumber. Aided by a stand of portable lights, rescue workers were pulling debris from what had been a bathroom, looking for survivors. The searchers knew that people often sought shelter in such compact, sturdy rooms. Tom and I offered to help, but the rescuers told us that almost everyone had been accounted for and that the search was just about over. I was surprised we were the only journalists on the scene, with the exception of a reporter from Midland. The remoteness of Saragosa and the roadblock were keeping others away.

We wandered around the rest of the night using the lights of the emergency crews as beacons. Many searchers were residents of Saragosa, and the pain and fatigue of the ordeal covered their faces.

The chain of events leading to this tragedy, we learned, had come together in the early morning hours.

Blueprint for Tragedy

Balloons are the first line of defense in severe weather forecasting. Nationwide, workers at National Weather Service (NWS) facilities launch the helium-filled orbs twice a day. Tethered to the balloons are radiosondes, shoebox-sized instrument packages that send data to a ground receiver.

As the radiosondes from west Texas and New Mexico ascended that morning, they detected increasing wind speeds (including "veering" winds which could eventually cause tornadoes) and dropping temperatures. Separately, a layer of warm, moist air was flowing northwest from the Gulf of Mexico, and a disturbance in the wind flow approached from the west.

At 3:20 p.m., these essential ingredients for a tornado merged and the first severe thunderstorm of the day formed in Reeves County, Texas, 23 miles northwest of Saragosa. The atmosphere was so volatile that these initial storms reached a height of about 50,000 feet—some 10,000 to 20,000 feet higher than the average thunderstorm—and quickly reached a level of danger, known as "severe." The NWS classifies a severe storm as having one or more of the following: winds of 58 miles per hour or higher; hail 3/4 inch or larger; tornado production; or a radar signature indicating severe weather.

At 4:35 p.m., the main storm collapsed and its top fell to 37,000 feet. But less than three hours later, it regenerated into an incredible supercell which topped out at 61,000 feet, just under 12 miles high. The NWS in Midland issued severe thunderstorm and flash flood warnings for the area.

At 7:46 p.m., storm spotters near Balmorhea (five miles south of Saragosa) reported the lower portion of the storm was beginning to rotate. The weather service issued a tornado warning at 7:54 p.m. as reports of rotating clouds continued.

Tornado ingredients brew in cumulonimbus clouds over west Texas.

The first tornado touchdown was reported by a DPS officer at 8:05 p.m., just to the west of Balmorhea. Nine minutes later, another tornado was reported on the ground about a mile and a half southwest of Saragosa. The tornado, consisting of a single, rapidly rotating column of air, or vortex, soon became a more sinister multi-vortex twister.

Rosendo Carrasco, a resident, had just left Guadalupe Hall in Saragosa after taking pictures of a pre-kindergarten graduation ceremony. For many of the people who attended the festivities, Carrasco's photos would be their last. As Carrasco headed home to Balmorhea, he saw what appeared to be a tornado forming in front of him and took a few photographs of it, unaware that it would shortly become a killer tornado.

At 8:14 p.m., just as the tornado was reaching its maximum intensity, residents of Saragosa were enjoying graduation ceremonies, oblivious of the imminent danger. The town, located in an area with few violent tornadoes, had no official storm spotter group, warning system or tornado siren.

The tornado, which had widened to over a quarter of a mile, soon churned through the town, disintegrating homes and hurling cars into buildings. Guadalupe Hall was reduced to a pile of concrete slabs, and 22 people, including many children, were dead. Within seconds, over two-thirds of Saragosa was demolished. The toll on Saragosa's population of 183 was 30 dead, 121 injured. This tornado was rated a 4 by NWS on its 1-5 "F" Scale, with winds estimated between 207 and 260 miles per hour.

Carrasco, a justice of the peace, returned to Saragosa following the tornado and performed the sad task of identifying the dead and assisting with rescue operations.

"Gosa"

The light of day provided a glimpse of an alien landscape that was once a small farming town. Few buildings were left intact. Walking along the highway, I noticed one section of pavement lifted away by the winds. Cars were ripped and torn apart, riddled with holes from flying debris, as if shot by a machine gun.

top: Destruction in Saragosa, Texas. May 1987.

left: Debris wrapped around a pole

right: A fork embedded in a debarked tree trunk

Several of these vehicles had been hurled over 900 feet into the surrounding fields. The few trees in town were reduced to stumps, completely bare of limbs and bark. Trees had pieces of metal or debris wrapped around the trunks. Dead animals, including a bloated horse, lay next to the highway. Tom and I snapped away, trying not to be too obvious as we made our way. Some residents resented our intrusion, but we did our work, often using our cameras as shields to deflect the pain and anger.

While I was standing near a pile of rubble pulling a nail out of my shoe, a tired woman, her pants and shirt tattered and stained, approached. I was fearful she would tell me how disgusted she was by my work. Instead, she said, "Come here, young man; I'll show you a photograph." She led me between several heaps of debris to a tree that had been completely de-barked. Deeply embedded into the stump was a bent kitchen fork. She saw the tornado coming and survived by seeking shelter in a small closet. She pointed to the scrap pile that was once her home. The entire structure was destroyed except for the small, sturdy closet where she rode out the twister. The fork, she said, was from her kitchen. I shot the fork and moved on.

By late morning, the remaining residents of Saragosa, many of whom had left for the night, returned. They sifted through the debris, crying, hugging each other, looking for anything salvageable. Those sifting through rubble might find a photograph or memento of a loved one who had died and would collapse into a tearful outburst. I came across a man kneeling by a pile of fractured lumber which was once a home. He was holding a child's doll, crying. Later, I found a mud-covered wallet lying on the ground and gave it to a DPS officer. The officer told me that the owner figured the twister had carried it away.

By noon the area was buzzing. Large satellite trucks and news crews lined the shoulders of the road. Behind one of the trucks, a sharply dressed anchorwoman was cursing to a cameraman about the mud on her new boots, as a family sifted through a scrap pile behind her.

A fleet of relief volunteers from churches and other organizations also poured into the town. One large disaster assistance truck pulled into town, complete with a list, painted on the side, of the major disasters at which it had assisted. News helicopters circled overhead as searchers made one last pass through the rubble.

We decided to leave as the media frenzy grew larger. Reporters were now following the victims' every move. Some aggressive news crews clearly crossed the borders of decency, and tempers flared. "Get the hell out of our town, you son-of-a bitch vulture," I heard one Saragosan yell at a reporter.

Before we left, I told Tom that I wanted to make a final pass over the south side of town.

"Have something in mind?" he asked.

“Yes, my closing image,” I said. “I’ve been looking for it all day. You know, that little green town name sign along the highway.” I knew it had taken a direct hit from the twister. I imagined it stuck in the side of a building, or in some other symbolic place.

After searching a few minutes on the far south end of town, where the tornado came roaring in, I found my shot. Covered with mud, in a field near the highway, was just half of the sign: “gosa.”

Magnificent Obsession

Over the next two days we chased storms in west Texas with limited success. These first-time twister-chasing episodes were marked by frustrating and dangerous events. We often became disoriented and confused by magnificent storm features that dwarfed anything that we had seen in Arizona. And with Saragosa still fresh on our minds, we were fearful a tornado would appear from a suspicious cloud and kill us. On the 24th, while driving next to a storm near Abilene, Texas, we watched people run to their tornado shelters when a dark cloud passed overhead. The cloud pressurized the interior of the car for a moment and popped our ears. It rattled our wits but did no other damage.

We also discovered that chasing is an expensive venture. And there were no guarantees our photographs would make any money. With little or no chase budget, we cut corners whenever possible. In lieu of paying for lodging, we spent cold nights sleeping (or trying to sleep) on reclined car seats. We even skipped meals to buy film or gas. To extend our chase time and save money, marathon drives of eighteen hours straight were not uncommon.

Remainder of Saragosa’s town sign

One thing was apparent: finding a tornado and staying alive while pursuing it would require time, money, patience and more knowledge. I also realized that my new pursuits would involve horrid scenes like Saragosa. As a journalist, I had seen many forms of death. But this was different. What I had witnessed before were accidents, shootings and crime—the havoc man causes to man. This was nature at its aggressive worst. Random. Unpredictable. Merciless.

Back in Tucson, my thoughts turned to my job woes and the upcoming monsoon season. I had won a television in a raffle but decided to sell it to support my chasing. With the money, I bought a new camera—a camera that would play a pivotal role in my career.

During the 1987 monsoon, I spent all my free time on the deserted hills surrounding Tucson, shooting my first professional lightning images. From the second week in June through the end of August, I scheduled my work shifts and even my social life around the monsoon. The month of May was now devoted entirely to the Plains.

The weather had begun to dictate my life.

Dave

Chase Log: May 20, 1988.
National Weather Service Office, Wichita Falls, Texas.

As we pulled into the parking lot, we saw it.

The world's most famous storm chase vehicle. It was not a high-tech truck with a zillion antennas, but a plain 1979 light silver Volkswagen Rabbit, with a single magnetic CB antenna stuck on the roof.

No one would have given this car a second look, except for a couple of excited storm chasers, who had just seen it on a *National Geographic* television special concerning tornado chasers. One quick look at the Virginia license plate, IN-FLOW, confirmed its authenticity. (The customized plate refers to the winds which feed into a tornado.) I snuck a quick picture.

"Yep," I said excitedly to Tom, "that's his car. I can't believe it; we're finally going to meet Dave!" This vehicle belonged to David Hoadley, one of the pioneer storm chasers and a legend that two rookies, on their second expedition into the Alley, were dying to meet.

When we walked into the office, Dave, in customary business dress, including a tie, was seated at a table completing his morning forecast. We stood back and observed as he prepared his forecast plot, using his own renowned formula, meticulously developed since the beginning of his chase days in 1956. Since then, Dave's forecasting skills have rewarded him with over 80 tornadoes and countless funnels. We recognized Dave from the television show and introduced ourselves.

Dave, a stickler for detail, asked how we spelled our names and included them in his notes. He courteously answered our questions about the day's forecast. "Somewhere near Abilene, Texas, looks good," he advised, peering at a pad containing technical data indecipherable to us.

"Oh ... yes ... sure does ... no doubt ... ," we responded, trying to conceal our ignorance.

Dave's well-known attention to detail and ability to rapidly calculate numbers is not surprising. He works as a budget analyst for the government and uses vacation time to chase. His yearnings to witness tornadoes are driven by scientific curiosity and a thirst for travel and adventure. Dave's unusual zeal for "the chase" is rooted in his own philosophy. He once stated in a television interview: "For me, tornadoes are a kind of natural wonder. They are about the most awesome thing that you can see, and they're one of the most spectacular forces of nature. It's almost magical in a

left: Warren Faidley with storm clouds in the background

top: Dave Hoadley being taped by a news crew during a chase in west Texas

way when it comes down, because so many things must go right in the atmosphere, and the timing has to be just right, even at the peak of the tornado season. To catch one of these things is an unforgettable experience. Once you see one you'll never forget it."

We left the weather office and headed down the highway. I noticed Dave's car in front of us. "Slow down," I said to Tom. "I don't want him to think we're following him." Dave would become a good friend, and we would sometimes join forces and "follow" each other during chases.

Chase Pioneers

Among the early hobby chasers, besides Dave, is Roger Jensen. Roger conducted his first storm chase in the summer of 1953 when his father drove him to a thunderstorm near Fargo, North Dakota. He was hooked after that.

He began photographing every storm he could find. His photography included everything from a mile-wide tornado to a softball-sized hailstone, which, incidentally, was one of the largest hailstones documented in the state. He once described his "ideal" storm to Dave Hoadley as "a spectacular 60,000-70,000 foot high thunderstorm, moving in from the west, with grapefruit-sized hailstones and spectacular mammatus clouds, [which] then drifts off to the southeast through an evening palette of orange, coral, rose and red." Mammatus clouds are dramatic, sac-like protrusions found on the underside of a storm.

Another pioneer chaser considered by many to be the true "father of storm chasing," is Neil B. Ward. In the early 1950s, Ward had already shown the signs of a man hooked on vortices. During family vacations in the Southwest, he would watch for dust devils. If he happened to see one nearby, he would take the family on an impromptu chase, driving the car towards the dust cloud. It was also during this period that Ward began to chase thunderstorms, occasionally inviting his neighbors to ride along.

On May 4, 1961, Ward conducted one of the most important storm chases of his life. After making arrangements to ride in an Oklahoma Highway Patrol unit, he began tracking a storm that produced a large, multiple-vortex tornado near Geary, Oklahoma. Using the patrol car's radio, he relayed information directly to the Weather Bureau in Oklahoma City. His detailed documentation and reports were able to correlate the infamous "hook" echo seen on weather radar with his real-time observations of the tornado. This memorable chase proved just how critical the role is that chasers play in severe weather research.

Ward became one of the nation's leading tornado research scientists and designed a laboratory tornado simulator that eventually produced the world's first simulated multiple vortices.

While chasers like Hoadley, Jensen and Ward were tracking storms during the early 1950s, the government soon realized that the public was in need of an early warning system for dangerous weather. In 1952, the Weather Bureau (renamed National Weather Service in 1967) organized the Severe Local Storm Forecasting Unit in Washington, D.C., and the first tornado forecasts were issued. In 1959, the first weather radar was commissioned, and in 1960, the first weather satellite, TIROS I, was launched. It was also during this period that local "spotter" networks were established. As a consequence, the first volunteer chasers/weather watchers were organized.

In 1964, the National Severe Storms Laboratory (NSSL) was established by the federal government in Norman, Oklahoma, to work in conjunction with the University of Oklahoma Department of Meteorology. The goals of the NSSL were to advance the understanding of thunderstorms and to improve detection of severe weather. In 1972, "The Tornado Intercept Project" or TIP, was initiated, and the nation's first group of scientific tornado chasers was organized. On April 14, 1972, the first chase day for TIP, Neil Ward was buried. He had died two days earlier of a heart ailment.

By the late 1970s, the NSSL chase teams had intercepted several tornadoes. Special "chase" vans were deployed, allowing researchers to track and collect scientific data and to film severe weather. Researchers also began applying Doppler radar, a breakthrough method for measuring internal precipitation and wind velocities.

Spotter and chaser reports again proved important in correlating radar signatures—the identifying patterns on the radar screen—to actual weather phenomena.

In 1977, Howard Bluestein, the guru of contemporary scientific tornado chasers, began his research at NSSL. He set out to answer the "big question" that has plagued scientists and chasers for years: Why do some thunderstorms produce tornadoes while others do not? From 1981 through 1983, his small group of chasers worked with a device nicknamed "TOTO." (The Totable Tornado Observatory, named after Dorothy's dog from *The Wizard of Oz*.) TOTO was a 400-pound package of weather-sensing instruments encased in a protective shell. It was designed to be placed in the path of a tornado and collect data while surviving the winds. Despite three chase seasons, TOTO was only brushed by a passing tornado. Scientists decided that placing the cumbersome device in the path of a tornado was

Supercell storm, eastern New Mexico

dangerous, if not impossible. In 1987, Bluestein and his chase team began using a portable Doppler radar for close-up storm measurements.

It was not until the late 1970s that the modern concept of "recreational" or "hobbyist" storm chasing evolved. In 1977, Dave Hoadley founded *Stormtrack*, a self-published journal for chasers. It includes everything from chaser news to detailed meteorological discussions about severe weather development. Dave's sense of humor was exemplified in a comic strip that he created for the publication entitled: "Funnel Funny." The strip poked fun at everything from chasers stuck in muddy fields to tornado-like characters sitting around tables joking about eluding chasers.

For over 30 years, the world of storm chasers was small and intimate, a pursuit of people who respected the storms and those who lived in their paths. It was a labor of love conducted on empty farm roads where chasers were simply regarded as passing tourists. This could not last.

Diamonds and Emerald Fields

Chase Log: May 30, 1988. Eastern New Mexico.

It was our second tornado chase season. We reached eastern New Mexico in the late afternoon just in time to witness the transformation of towering white cumulus clouds into a spectacular supercell storm at the Texas/New Mexico border. Tom Willett, my chase partner, occasionally pointed his camera out the window and fired a few frames. Unlike the tragic aftermath of Saragosa, this was heaven. We watched the sky overflow with color-laden energy, spilling out over the desolate Plains, destined to harm no one.

We followed the storm until it disintegrated south of Portales, New Mexico. While we were on the side of the road taking a last pre-sunset look at the clouds, an old green pickup pulled up next to us.

A large man clad in blue farmers' overalls, black horn-rimmed glasses and a straw cowboy hat, yelled over at us. "It was a hell of a storm for a while."

"Sure was," I shouted back.

He looked us over and asked, "You boys out here chasing storms?"

"Yes," I replied assertively. "We're storm photographers from Tucson."

"Now ain't that something, all the way from Tucson," he said, shaking his head. "We get a lot of the big ones [storms] around here." He glanced north. "Boy, it looks like there's a couple of whoppers up there near Clovis, and I'll bet they get their butts kicked up there."

"Yes, it sure does," I replied, "but I don't think we could catch them before dark."

He told us that he worked for a New Mexico petroleum company and "spotted" storms as a hobby. In fact, he was just one of the thousands of local weather spotters throughout the Plains who keep an eye on suspicious weather and report anything hazardous to the Weather Service by ham radio or mobile phone.

Had this been any other afternoon, the royal blue sky would have only been a graceful transition between day and night. But tonight, the two magnificent, pure

Sunset-crowned storm clouds in New Mexico

white thunderheads in the northeast contrasted so vividly against the sky that the entire horizon was transformed into a beautiful and majestic scene.

As the towering storms drew closer, the sky darkened, and the clouds became translucent from constant internal lightning flashes. Some lightning bolts leaped from the top of the storms, reaching toward the heavens. The top of the westernmost storm was bathed in a wondrous golden glow from some distant sunset, while overhead, a few bright stars shone like diamonds set on the storm's amber crown. We sat quietly and simply absorbed the show as it unfolded over the endless emerald fields which flowed to-and-fro from the breeze.

Then it dawned on me; this was the essence of chasing. I had begun to fall in love with the Plains. And fortunately, the entire scene was just out of the range of our lenses. Otherwise, we might have lost the moment scurrying to photograph it.

Storms continued to expand throughout eastern New Mexico and west Texas during the early evening. One of the storms we saw building at sunset eventually dropped a tornado outside of Clovis. Fatigued by our long, exciting day, we decided to spend the night at the cheapest place we could find in Clovis. We located a bargain-basement hotel with the customary dilapidated pool filled with brown water and rooms that rated a "10" on the "chaser's funky smell" list.

We spent the evening listening to Tom's weather-alert radio, as the National Weather Service issued warnings for storms in our area. This was the first time in our adult lives that either one of us had stayed in a place where there was a threat of being pulverized by a twister while we were asleep. The radio's alert tone, a loud siren, went off several times that night, signaling that a severe warning was being issued. We talked ourselves into believing tornadoes were coming down all over the place. The number of warnings tapered off after midnight, and the excitement faded into fatigue. Tom decided to leave the radio on just in case. I drifted off into an uneasy sleep.

All at once the siren went off accompanied by a string of horrible crashing sounds. I sprang from bed and stood dazed. Tom sat up in his bed as we both considered our next move. My mind raced. Should I pull the mattress from the bed and use it as a cover in the bathtub as someone suggested on the weather radio earlier that evening? Should I dare look out the window and be slashed by flying glass?

Just when I decided to move towards the bathroom, expecting the walls to come crashing down, the noise stopped. We discovered the source of our fright: our air conditioner unit had suffered some major mechanical malfunction at precisely the same time as the alarm sounded for a distant county. Two novice chasers had much to learn about life in the Alley.

We left the next morning for Tucson. I was totally hooked on chasing, but I didn't have the vaguest idea of how I could make a living from it.

On June 23, 1988, I walked into the newspaper office, smiled, walked to a typewriter and pecked out "I quit."

No regrets. The monsoon was just a few weeks away, and by then I had a plan, of sorts.

The vast horizons of the Plains as pre-storm clouds gather

FIRE AND WATER

CHASE LOG: AUGUST 20, 1988.
10 MILES WEST OF TUCSON.

No sooner had I clicked the shutter when a round of loud gunfire rang out, and bullets ricocheted on the rocks just above my head. I hit the ground and lay as flat as I could as more shots whizzed overhead. OK, so chasing storms is dangerous, but no one ever warned me about gunfire.

I had traveled west this particular day, as on most monsoon afternoons, with the hope that the rising storm cells would grow into a thunderstorm. I had lucked out—well, sort of.

The moment I arrived at the base of a small hill off Highway 86, I lugged my equipment up to a rocky ledge, set up my tripods and checked the exposure with a hand-held light meter. Everything was framed in my viewfinder as I anxiously waited for daylight to fade and for the storm to start dropping lightning bolts.

To my joy, the pale orange sky erupted into a classic Arizona, pinkish-red sunset. Crystal-blue lightning bolts began to weave their

previous pages: Thunderhead over western Tucson, colored, in part, by ash in the atmosphere produced by the eruption of Mt. Pinatubo

way through the growing storm's cauliflower-shaped crown, giving the appearance of a giant brain coming to life.

The first bolt of cloud-to-ground lightning caught my eye. I reached to open the camera shutters—and then, whoosh, an odd sound overhead. Must be some kind of bird, I thought. I looked up to see hundreds of bats darting from a large crack in the rocks a few feet above my head. The mysterious sound was the massive flapping of bat wings, many uncomfortably close to my head.

But even bats couldn't distract me for long. My attention was diverted from the flying fur balls when a small lightning bolt leaped from the side of the thunderhead and hit the desert. I opened the shutter and began exposing the cloud.

Suddenly, there was a new distraction—this one potentially far more lethal. Gunfire.

My instinct was to yell, to warn shooters that someone (me) was perched on the side of the hill. But since I did not know the reason for their shooting, I kept mum, fearing their next response might be to fire at the source of the voice.

A lightning bolt hits the desert near Green Valley, Arizona.

The gunfire stopped and was followed by a round of loud whooping voices. I crawled to the tripod, reached up and closed the shutter as a gigantic bolt dropped from the storm. "Those sons of bitches!" I cursed. "If I missed that shot, I'm gonna be real pissed off!"

The storm produced another brilliant lightning strike, and, almost on cue, the shooting resumed. Between rounds of fire, I maneuvered up to the top of the ledge and peeked over the rocks. Three cowboys, complete with hats and six shooters, were downing beer and blasting away at empty cans and an old television set on the side of the hill just below me. Their voices—and their aim—made it clear they were totally inebriated. I was glad I hadn't yelled moments before.

The storm continued its light show as the sky turned a dark blood-red. The gunfire continued and now included an occasional shotgun blast mixed with unnerving screams of "Kiss my ass" and "Yee-ha." The purpose of this male bonding became evident when one of the cowboys cried out profanities about how "Suzy" had done him wrong.

When the firing subsided, I headed to the opposite side of the hill to get a longer shutter cable from my car. I wanted to limit my exposure to the bullets. I'm the first to acknowledge that there are dangers in chasing storms, but dodging bullets is not supposed to be among them. When I reached the car and deactivated the alarm, I had an idea. I reset the alarm and kicked a tire, setting off the loud siren. I then yelled as loud as I could, in a deep authoritative voice, "JUST WHAT THE HELL IS GOING ON HERE!"

The shooting stopped.

I figured that the drunk outlaws would suffer some paranoia from the loud sound. I raced back up the hill, laughing under my breath as I watched a squeaky old pickup, without lights, make a quick dash to the highway.

When I reached the tripod, I advanced the shutter, knowing that the last frame, which had been exposed for several minutes, was a waste. I was none too happy about that, but the chuckle from watching the fleeing cowboys had made it worth my while. The truck appeared to have become stuck in the sandy desert about a mile away.

I continued *my* brand of shooting until the lightning diminished. As I was packing my equipment, another group of shooters, this time on motorcycles, pulled up to a pond across the highway. They began prolonged firing at toads in the water. That was enough of the desert serenity for that day. I was out of there.

Or was I?

I started down the hill only to freeze in my steps as I heard the unmistakable buzz of a rattlesnake. I moved gingerly in the near darkness and turned my head to the left. There it was. Coiled on a rock about five feet away, the snake was just out of striking range. I hurried along. This was my day for harassment, first from man, then from nature. I did manage to take one wonderful image of the storm—and I was given a nickname "Cloud Stalker ™" by an Apache Indian friend after he heard my story.

Photograph accomplished between "bats" and "bullets"

Out of the Blue

Thunder's flapping wings and the flaming arrows shot by the Lightning People terrorize the Cloud People into making rain for the thirsty earth.

Zia Indian folklore

Lightning is a storm chaser's greatest natural danger. It is unlike other storm phenomena such as tornadoes and hurricanes. Lightning will seek out its target, attracted to even the smallest piece of metal like a steel tripod or a metal zipper on a pair of pants.

Once, while shooting a thunderstorm near Willcox, Arizona, my aluminum tripod suddenly became electrified, and the shock numbed my hands. I took a few steps away from the tripod, fell to the ground and covered my head, expecting a lightning charge to make its way through the tripod. Just as I lowered my body, a terrific lightning bolt zipped overhead, leaping from cloud to cloud. A loud thunderclap followed. My hands ached for hours, but I was thankful the bolt didn't make it to the ground.

The physics involved in lightning are amazing. The lightning channel, which we see as a large, bright white column, is in reality only about an inch in diameter. The energy from a lightning strike can reach upward of 100,000 amperes. By way of comparison, the average electrical house circuit carries 30 amps. The temperature of the channel can reach nearly 50,000 degrees Fahrenheit, which is about five times hotter than the surface of the sun. Lightning is also a common occurrence: the earth is hit about 100 times per second by lightning bolts. Lightning kills an average of 200 people annually.

Lightning also acts in strange ways. Mary Clamser of Oklahoma City was struck by the residual energy from a lightning strike to an outside satellite dish while flushing a toilet. The shock was so intense that it threw her into an adjacent room. Several weeks later she was up and walking again. Normally, she would have been deemed merely a lucky survivor; what is so remarkable about her story, however, is that she had not walked for years because of multiple sclerosis.

Another unusual story involved park ranger Roy C. Sullivan, who was known as the "human lightning rod." During a career of working in the forest, Sullivan was hit by lightning in 1942, '69, '70, '72, '73, '76 and finally on June 26, 1977. In the 1942 strike, he lost a big toe. In 1969 his eyebrows were singed. Twice, his hair caught fire. Despite his incredible encounters with lightning, he died a natural death in 1982. Curiously, my mother cut out a newspaper article about Roy after his third hit in 1970 and gave it to me. No underestimating Mama's intuition.

When I started working near lightning in 1982, I had neither knowledge nor appreciation of the physics or dangers of lightning. My lack of understanding—and

left: Unusual shot of cloud-to-cloud and air-discharge lightning near Picacho, Arizona

top: Lightning hits a copper smelter in San Manuel, Arizona.

fear—made my earliest adventures with thunderstorms life-threatening. I nearly kissed the earth good-bye on several occasions in my initial challenges of the storm gods.

In one terrifying instance, captured on a video camera near Marana, Arizona, a renegade bolt struck the ground 10 feet from my tripod. The footage was eventually shown on a *National Geographic Explorer* special. "This small bolt could have killed Faidley," says the narrator.

On another occasion, also near Marana, a lightning bolt hit power lines above my car as I shot a dust storm. The strike sent arcing wires on top of my car. The blinding flash and ensuing thunderclap startled me so much that I lifted myself out of the seat and banged my head on the roof. Appropriately, "I Fall to Pieces" by Patsy Cline faded out for a moment on the radio as the lightning's energy distorted the airwaves. It took a minute for my sight to be restored so I could drive safely away from burning wires that surrounded my car and a major brush fire ignited by the wires.

My escapades into the desolate regions of southern Arizona provided no shortage of spooky adventures and humor. Among my encounters: armed drug runners, scorpions and flash floods.

Once, I was shooting a storm about midnight at a ranch near Sonoita, Arizona, when a magnificent lightning bolt flashed overhead and hit somewhere behind me. It was so close that my hair stood on end. I turned, half-bent in fright. After the last echo of rolling thunder faded from the nearby hills, there was silence again—except for a peculiar noise that became louder and louder. The noise was nothing I had heard before.

---

top: Lightning strikes close to Faidley's camera tripod and car, captured on a remote video camera. August 1990. (See bolt at far right.)

right: Lightning strike to the Catalina Mountains, north of Tucson

The mystery became unbearable. My pulse quickened with fear, but my curiosity won over. I grabbed a small flashlight and walked down a dirt road toward the sound. About 50 yards down the road, the noise rose to a higher pitch. For some damn reason, it seemed to be coming from the sky. I swear I saw something red flash high above for a split second. My flashlight beam dimmed to a weak, useless glow. The wind picked up and a light rain started to fall.

Normally, my imagination doesn't interfere with my reasoning. However, earlier in the evening, I had tuned in an AM radio talk show on UFO abductions. Most happen on nights in the middle of nowhere, the experts said. Well, Sonoita is pretty close to being the middle of nowhere, and the night was dark, and those lightning flashes were making the cacti look as though they were moving. I went back to the car.

Just as I turned and walked a few feet, there was a screech, then a loud metallic crash. I jumped to the side of the road, caught my foot on a rock and fell into the desert with my heart pounding in my ears. Fortunately, I fell right between two large, needle-sharp, cholla cacti. I paused, listened, stood and looked around me, expecting to glimpse the saucer people with their humongous dark eyes. Instead, there was dead silence, except for the rain. The eerie sound disappeared. I continued on, casting glances over my shoulder every few steps.

I packed the gear in the car and drove toward the highway. But curiosity was not only nagging me, it was hounding me. I turned the car around and went to solve the mystery.

I wasn't sure exactly where to go. The rain was now steady and I hunted for the two cacti, but there were so many that it was impossible to pinpoint where I'd been. I hunted for 15 minutes, then gave up and turned the car around. And my headlights solved the mystery.

Thirty feet off to the right side of the road stood a metal windmill tower, its circular vanes missing. I backed up and flicked on the brights to survey the ground below the tower. Sure enough. The vanes lay at the tower base. The tower had been hit by the lightning strike, and the damaged vanes had sparked, clanged and emitted a metallic groan.

GILBERT

CHASE LOG: SEPTEMBER 15-17, 1988. SAN ANTONIO, TEXAS.

My brain was on strike. Yet I could clearly smell the fresh, air-dried sheets on my bed and feel my head sinking into the soft feather pillows. Click, click, click. If only I had those ruby-red slippers.

I was thoroughly exhausted. Every movement, every thought required a second effort. After 48 hours and 900 miles of hectic driving along the Texas Gulf coast, it took every ounce of concentration to make it back to San Antonio.

I had traveled along the coast the last two days, trying to intercept Gilbert, a hurricane billed as the "most intense in recorded Atlantic history." On September 13, Gilbert, while churning in the western Caribbean Sea, had indeed broken the western hemisphere's record minimum sea-level pressure (26.22 millibars). On the 14th, Gilbert slammed into Mexico's Yucatan Peninsula near Cancun and Cozumel. Packing sustained winds of 175 miles per hour, Gilbert became one of the most powerful hurricanes ever to strike the North American continent. After leaving a trail of death and destruction in the Yucatan, the storm moved into the Gulf of Mexico and headed westward. Like most hurricanes, its path was uncertain, but a strike to the Texas coast was a good possibility.

left: Dual-branched lightning strikes Tucson.

My premier as a hurricane chaser began with an airline trip—my first air-assisted chase—from Tucson to San Antonio. I then drove a rental car into the wee hours to Corpus Christi. From there, I headed to Brownsville.

Taking this trip was a tough choice. I had been away from the paper for only three months, and I had no discretionary funds in my tiny budget. Pulling hundreds of dollars out of my savings to chase an unpredictable hurricane, and a potential dud, was difficult.

I pondered what photos I hoped to take as I drove the lonely 158-mile stretch of Highway 77 from Corpus Christi to Brownsville. This flat expanse, which paralleled the coast, was deserted.

"I have traveled more than 70 miles, and I've only passed one or two cars," I dictated to my tape recorder. "I must be extremely careful here, I haven't seen any gas stations open, and I fear that the low-lying road will quickly become a raging river if the storm hits. Information is scarce, and I'm not sure where Gilbert is going inland. This is damn uncomfortable."

As I approached Harlingen, the wind and rain became so intense that I could barely stay on the road. Fear, lack of experience, some flying debris and water rising over the highway all contributed to my decision to scuttle my Brownsville plans and head north to a safer inland highway. I began the tiresome drive to San Antonio to stay with my brother, Darrell. I was dejected, aware that this trip would not produce the hurricane images I so desperately needed.

Gilbert's ferocious core missed the U.S. coastline, striking the northeast coast of Mexico, just south of Brownsville, Texas. In all, over 300 people had been killed by the storm—so far.

Although Gilbert seemed long gone, a remnant of its incredible energy moved into south Texas. My pursuit of this hurricane wasn't over.

I collapsed on my brother's sofa and awoke in the early morning to the sound of sirens. They

Flood waters from Hurricane Gilbert surge over the highway near Corpus Christi, Texas.

had become incessant. Darrell turned on the television. Gilbert had left its mark. A tornado had ripped through an apartment complex less than a mile away, killing two people. My hurricane hunt was transformed into a tornado chase, and we spent the morning traveling the rolling countryside trying to witness one of the more than 30 (mostly rain-shrouded) tornadoes that hit Texas.

The circle of chasing was now complete. I had pursued everything from a dust devil to a tropical cyclone. Gilbert had not produced the images I wanted, but I knew there would be other, even more vicious, hurricanes to pursue.

September wound to a close, and the chase season ended. I returned to the world of part-time photography with an eye on saving enough money to return to the Alley in May. I worked part-time as a photography instructor and shot weddings on weekends.

I considered the idea of creating my own stock photography agency, specializing in weather images. A stock photography agency is a business arrangement where an agent (or a photographer) maintains a massive archive of images and sells reproduction rights to clients. Agencies split profits 50/50. Stock photography offers professionals the opportunity to shoot what they want, when they want and how they want. This concept fit my independent psyche like a glove. But I didn't have the capital to start a business. I was a maverick photographer who chased bad weather. Few knew who I was or what I did for a living.

This would change in a flash.

Damage from a tornado caused by the remnants of Hurricane Gilbert, San Antonio, Texas.

Bloody Palms, Black Widows and the Shot of a Lifetime

Chase Log: October 16, 1988.
Tucson, Arizona.

The storm season was over, and I was downing a beer late in the afternoon with Don Robertson, a journalism buddy. I was contemplating my business plans, unaware that my destiny was brewing in a storm 30 miles east of Tucson.

By chance, I glanced out the back window of my apartment and, to my shock, saw an eastern sky filled with the sharp edge of an anvil cloud. "Where on earth did this monster come from?" I asked. Nothing had been forecast. Hell, the season was over.

I darted to the phone and called the Tucson National Weather Service office, which confirmed that this storm was considered "severe" and was in excess of 50,000 feet.

Rare, massive, single discharge taken from a mountaintop near Tucson

It was approaching the city in a hurry and was producing "an unusual amount of lightning," the meteorologist said. I looked out the window to reassure myself, then called Tom, my chase partner, to see if he had laid eyes on this latecomer. "One more of your rotten jokes?" he asked, as I listened to him move toward a window and look out. "What the . . . there is a fricking storm out there!" he said.

Gathering my gear was no easy task, since I wasn't ready for a storm in the middle of October. Halfway down the steps, I realized I had left my film in the refrigerator. In his best John Wayne impression, Don wished me, "Happy hunting, amigo," and I was gone. I raced across town toward the storm, now classified a "severe thunderstorm."

The post-sunset sky was giving way to an exceptional bluish hue, providing a stark contrast to the white-capped storm clouds. As the light faded even more, I could see the storm was infused with brilliant, constant lightning. Each time a neon-white bolt crashed to the earth, I swore, frustrated at my tardiness.

I knew southern Arizona inside out and had scouted at least 100 locations that offered a range of perspectives. My mind sifted through my location index as I drove. Finally, I opted for a highway underpass on the east edge of town. I had shot from this location just once, but it had offered a variety of angles that included an unobstructed view of the east and an industrial backdrop to the west, including numerous silver-colored fuel storage tanks. A trade-off of risks: the underpass would shelter me from the storm, but damp or humid shelter, such as caves, also carry the deadly current of a lightning strike. That is, I'd get the shot I wanted, then die of electrocution.

I pulled to a sliding stop in the underpass as a series of powerful lightning bolts hit the ground just a few miles away. I jumped from the car, grabbed my gear and began the careful climb up a steep, 50-foot section of concrete that led to a ledge under the highway. The embankment was covered by rough, sharp concrete. Any slip would mean damaging my equipment—and losing lots of skin.

I scaled the embankment to the war drums of thunder and lightning. In a minute, I had set a camera atop a tripod and was shooting. The timing was perfect. Within 30 seconds, a spectacular bolt leaped out of the cloud a mile away and hit the ground next to an air traffic control tower at Davis Monthan Air Force Base.

It was like winning a prize fight in the first round. “Yes!” I shouted, my fist high in the air, the crash of thunder echoing all about. It was a strange scene, and only then was I aware that people in a car below had been watching my behavior. They could only have suspected a madman was on the loose. My rejoicing was cut short, however, as the sky opened up and bombarded me with heavy rain and wind. Small lightning bolts, which can portend a ground strike, leaped from cloud to cloud. My eastern view was now cut off by the storm, and I had but one choice. I would have to move to the opposite end of the underpass and shoot toward the storage tanks.

The dilemma? How to get there.

I could shimmy down the embankment, walk down the road and climb back up to the other end. Or, I could take a riskier shortcut and walk along a two-foot-wide ledge that continued for 100 feet or so. I chose the shortcut.

Rain began to pound the embankment walls, making me doubt my decision-making skills once again. There was only a four-foot clearance from the bottom of the ledge to the top of the underpass, so I crouched and began a duck-walk, grabbing steel gutters to keep my balancing act successful. The storm blasted away, and lightning illuminated the underpass like the best strobe flash. The thunder grew louder, and my march was going fine until—cobwebs!

Lightning strikes near the Davis Monthan Air Force Base traffic control tower as a severe storm approaches Tucson.

I had grabbed a handful of thick cobwebs from amongst the steel gutters. I recoiled in terror and beat the cobwebs against my pants leg. I had thought of occupational hazards—but not this. I flipped on my penlight. To my horror, rainwater was seeping through cracks in the concrete supports. The rain was driving hundreds of black widow spiders out in an angry mob. Crack. Boom!!! I cowered as a tremendous bolt of lightning hit overhead, followed by a cracking sound and thunderclap that roared through the underpass. The shaking set off my car alarm. I lost my grip for a second, and my penlight went rolling down the embankment.

The next bolt was likely to hit on the west side, and I would have one fleeting chance to get it. I used my tripod as a club and a walking stick and forged a path through the cobwebs, frantically swatting at spiders on my clothing. A pale flash in the low clouds reflected off the shiny storage tanks in a metallic blue. "What a fantastic color." I moved on.

I had 10 feet left to reach the west side, and I was now out of spiderland. I decided to stop and shoot west. The air sizzled with energy, and my instincts said something was going to happen—soon.

In order to shoot the tank farm from the best angle, I would have to move down the embankment a few more feet. In a squatting position, I used the rubber soles on my shoes and the palms of my hands as brakes. I set up tripods, checked the scene through the view finders, cleaned the rain off the front lenses, and with a long cable release, set the cameras' shutters to f/16. My strategy would be to expose for several minutes. I was too easy a target for the lightning, so I climbed back up the embankment a few feet.

At once, a blinding white flash and a loud crackling sound filled the night, as if the sky were being torn apart. A violent concussion lifted me off the ground for a moment, followed by a thunderclap that hit me like a bomb blast. There was a pungent smell, similar to burning plastic. My car alarm sounded again, and within seconds, a louder siren began to wail from the tank farm.

My senses were overloaded. I lost my footing and started to slide down the embankment directly toward the tripods and cameras. Though dazed, I knew damn well that if I slid into the cameras, the images would be blurred. Using my palms, shoes and the seat of my pants as emergency brakes, I forced my weight against the rough concrete and came to a stop straddling the tripods.

With the steadiest hand that I could manage, I reached up and closed the cameras' shutters.

Sirens blared away at the tank farm. I half expected the tanks to blow sky-high. My palms were oozing blood. I advanced the film and opened the shutters again.

I stayed in the underpass until the storm was long gone. I wanted to collect my thoughts. I didn't know where the lightning had struck, but it had been close. When I closed my eyes, I could see a ghostly white vertical line.

I stopped at a convenience market on the way home for a beer. I was entitled to it. The clerk, who knew me from other post-storm encounters, asked what I had done to my pants and then noticed the blood on my hands. My sliding had worn a hole in the pants and my scraped hands looked like they were out of a cheap science fiction movie. "You wouldn't believe me if I told you," I said.

I spent an anxious few hours the next day as the color transparencies were developed. I felt like an expectant father as I paced the lobby of the lab. When the clerk brought my film out, I went through the unmounted roll, frame by frame. There was the lightning bolt near the tower, a wonderful image in itself. Then, after a few blank frames—set off accidentally during the spider encounter—I found what I was looking for.

Even then, I could not believe it. In the center of my 15-frame roll taken with my (raffle money) camera was a breathtaking lightning bolt, some 400 feet from the lens, striking a light pole in the foreground of the tank farm.

Eureka! An accomplishment that rivaled riding my bicycle into the center of a dust devil.

I had just taken the closest, highest-quality image of a lightning bolt striking an object. Ever. The temptation was to do a celebratory jig. I tucked the transparency away and went home. I was thrilled with my professional accomplishment but didn't for a minute suspect that my future was delicately embossed on that thin membrane of plastic.

---

following pages: Lightning strikes a light pole in an oil and gasoline tank farm, less than 400 feet from Faidley. Tucson, October 1988.

PENNIES FROM HEAVEN

My image became known as "Lightning vs. the Tank Farm," and it became a catalyst for my career. It would be the topic of a scientific paper by E. Philip Krider, Ph.D., one of the nation's renowned lightning physicists, and it would be further scrutinized, digitized and analyzed by scientists and journalists around the world.

In March of 1989, the photograph appeared in *Life* Magazine, which billed me as a "storm photographer." This launched a media frenzy. *National Geographic* called and wanted to produce a television special about my work. Tabloids featured me as the "Fearless Spider-Fighting Photog." I received a call from a Japanese game show that wanted to feature me on a "What's My Line"-type show, in which contestants try to guess a person's occupation.

Overnight, my life was changing. Propitious timing, too. I had but a month's worth of expenses left in my savings account, and this would be my moment to capitalize on the business end of my work. The next day I converted my small apartment's living/dining room into an office, purchased used file cabinets and ordered some business cards. I began answering the phone, "Good morning, Weatherstock®," a name I thought up while brainstorming in the bathtub the night before.

Fortunately, I did not have to ferret out clients. They came knocking. Even months after the *Life* story, my phone was ringing nonstop. Advertisers and magazine editors hunting for lightning and other weather-related images tracked me down. One Fortune 500 CEO (who thought that I had the "neatest job on earth") called to chat and ask if I had any pictures of "jagged mountain peaks" to use in his company's annual report.

"Yes, sir," I lied. "Weatherstock has extensive files of mountain images."

"Great," he responded, "send them right away."

I hung up, ran to my car and drove around shooting every jagged mountain peak I could find. Off went the pictures; in came Weatherstock's first official sale: $500.

On another occasion, a client was so desperate for a tornado shot—of which I had none—that he said cost was no factor. "And if you can't find one, create it as a special effect if you can," he requested.

"Don't worry," I said. No photographs anywhere. Time to improvise.

I called my girlfriend and told her I needed a used nylon stocking and a tampon tube. She thought I had some kinky, dark side, until I explained my plan for the props.

I filled the nylon with sawdust, forming it into a funnel shape, and used the wispy, dense cotton pulled from the tampon to fashion a dust swirl at the base of the tornado. A genuine storm transparency served as a backdrop. I shot the set with every combination of light I could think of to give it a realistic look.

I may have gone to extremes. I tried to spin the stocking using an electric drill, but the funnel spun out of control, burst open and filled my apartment with sawdust. I constructed a second twister, but while I was at lunch, it was attacked and destroyed by Yoda, my girlfriend's cat. The third vortex worked, and it looked like a real Texas twister. The client loved it. Ironically, the published image inspired a couple of amateur photographers with true-to-life tornado and storm images to call me, asking if I would represent them. Overnight I became a photographic stock agent and had acquired a more extensive file of photographs.

In the spring of 1989, I produced my first one-hour video on storm chasing and severe weather, entitled "Thunderstorm." The homemade tape included my own footage and chase footage from government sources. I placed small ads in magazines and specialty publications. Within a few weeks my mailbox was overflowing with order forms and checks.

I didn't have illusions about chasing storms in a Mercedes. But, on the other hand, this was notches above chasing dust devils on a bicycle.

Homemade tornado image

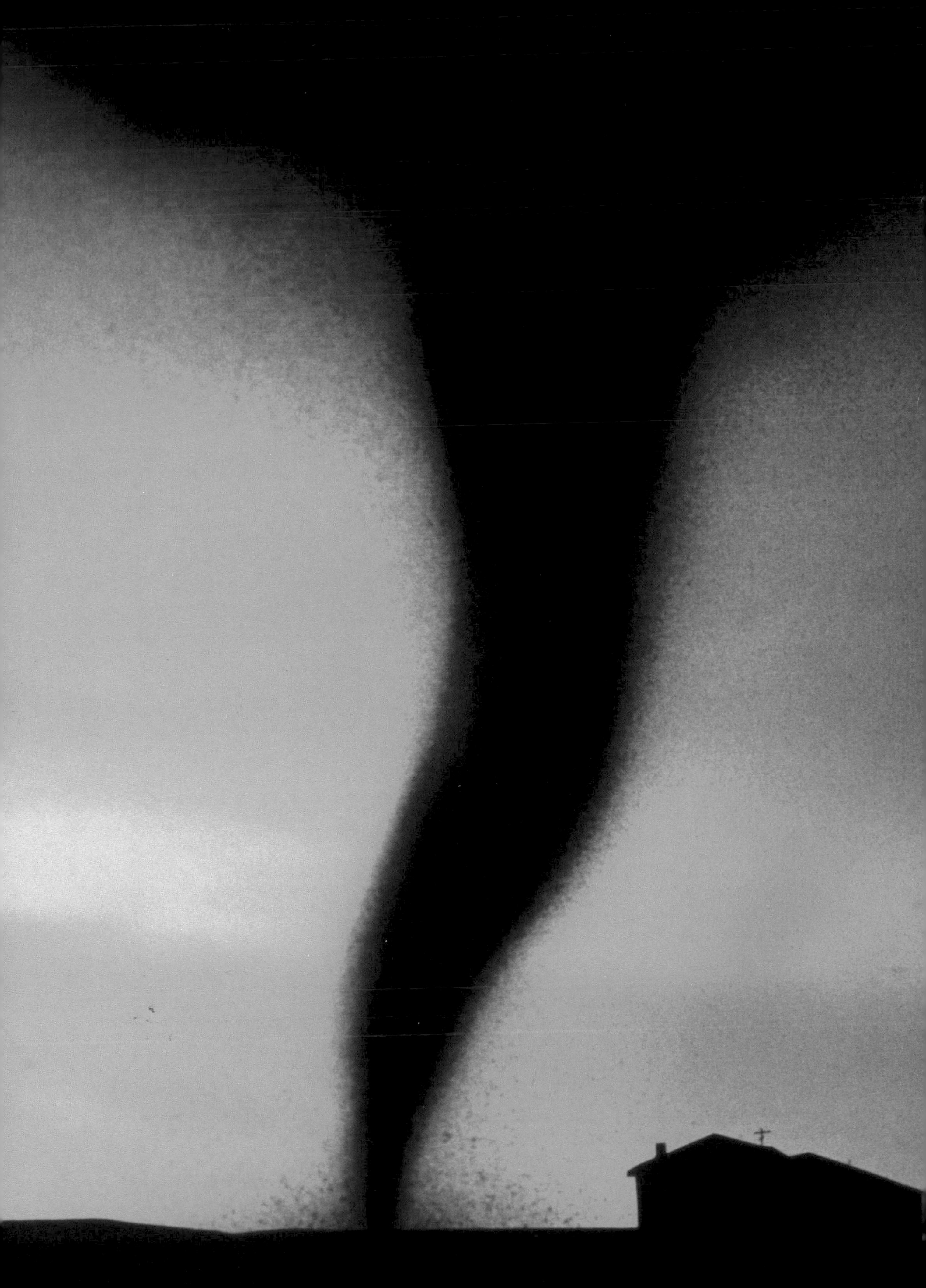

THE NATURE OF THE BEASTS

Tornadoes had eluded me.

Three years of chasing and I had yet to see one. I had witnessed numerous funnels, even a few suspect tornadoes wrapped in rain or darkness, but I had no definitive tornado on film or video. Nor did I have any idea that finding one would be so demanding, in time and brain power. What started as a challenge now blossomed into an all-out obsession. Spring of 1990 approached, and my mission in life was to find the perfect tornado and capture it on film.

Unfortunately, tornadoes don't announce themselves. Out of 100,000 thunderstorms that are reported each year in the U.S.,

A tornado looms near a farmhouse, northern Oklahoma. April 26, 1991. (Image digitally enhanced to show detail.)

approximately 1,000 tornadoes will be officially recorded, yet less than 50 percent are chaseable, and even fewer offer good photographic opportunities. The majority of twisters occur in the cloak of darkness, hide within the shadows of rain and/or hail or form with little forewarning. In addition, they often drop over remote, inaccessible landscapes and can flee at speeds of 40 to 60 mph. Others exist for a fleeting moment, under the average life span of 10 minutes. Often, the shape and color of the tornado is lost on film to poor contrast, severely diffused by mist from high humidity, or obscured by dust.

Then the hard part: once I found a photographable twister, I would need to get close enough to get my shots without becoming one of the 80 or more Americans annually (on average) who are killed by them. Besides a blessing of luck, I would have to become a precise forecaster if I was going to capture a tornado and live to chase again. It was that simple.

To that end, I spent countless hours looking over every relevant textbook, technical report, historical record, film and magazine article that I could find. When

I visited National Weather Service offices, I deluged my hosts with questions. I paid detailed attention to my own forecasts, making notes of my mistakes. I learned to use a computer to gain access to weather data and plot my own charts.

Perhaps the most important thing I learned during my observations was that the creation of a twister is an act of perfect timing. Environment and storm work together like a finely tuned machine. In order for substantial, chaseable storms to form, a number of atmospheric elements and events must merge at precisely the right time.

Of the hundreds of possible atmospheric elements and scenarios which may produce severe weather, three elements are always present on big, severe weather days: a sufficient amount of moisture (measured as the dew point), dynamics to lift the air (such as a low pressure system) and jet streams, which help, among other things, to create tornadic rotation within a storm by providing favorable wind shear.

Throughout the spring and early summer, it is not uncommon for this witch's brew to be present over the Plains. The only problem: such ingredients only come together in the proper sequence to create chaseable tornadoes on a few days. Ultimately, timing is the most decisive factor in the creation of severe weather. If a forecasted element is missing, weakens, or fails to fall into place at the right time, storms will not form, or they'll develop into short-lived freaks which aren't worth chasing. One of the most common examples of this problem occurs when the atmosphere is highly unstable during the afternoon hours, but the main dynamics arrive after dark causing a nighttime severe weather event. The timing factor occasionally works in the opposite manner. In fact, major severe weather events have occurred when one or more "missing" elements suddenly develop.

Fortunately, a few pieces of the chasing puzzle are no mystery. It is common knowledge that the most graphic tornadoes, and the highest frequency of tornadic events, occur from April to June, with the greatest concentration in the last two weeks of May and the first week of June. It is during this period that Gulf moisture works its way northward into the Plains, spring dynamics enter the region from the

left: Tornado, near Laverne, Oklahoma. May 15, 1991.

west, and jet stream winds race across the area. Thus, some severe weather "outbreak" events are apparent days in advance. There are also large-scale indications that rule out severe weather for days, or weeks, on end, such as massive areas of stable air.

The domain of the most awesome twisters on this planet is certainly no enigma. It is a region where the elements come together most often with explosive force. It's nicknamed "Tornado Alley."

The Alley

Tornado Alley has no official boundaries. Using government tornado occurrence statistics as geographic boundaries, it generally includes most of the central and east-central United States, bordered by western Kentucky to the east, and eastern Colorado toward the west. This region has the world's highest frequency of tornadoes, including "families" of violent tornadoes.

The eastern portions of the Alley have a particularly deadly reputation. For example: the "super outbreak" of April 3-4, 1974, produced 148 tornadoes that hit a thirteen-state area east of the Mississippi River. Winds in at least six of these tornadoes were estimated at more than 261 mph. (The average tornado has wind speeds of less than 150 mph.) More than 300 people died, and over 6,000 injured. The most devastating U.S. tornado to date occurred in the Alley on March 18, 1925. The "Tri-State" tornado remained on the ground for an incredible 219 miles, killed

above: Supercell storm over Tornado Alley, seen from a high-altitude jet

695 people and injured over 2,000, in Missouri, Illinois and Indiana. Several towns in the path of this tornado were completely destroyed.

What strikes me as remarkable about these figures is how *low* they are, given the potential for disaster. Even with Doppler radar and networks of spotters, many residents of Tornado Alley are surprisingly apathetic. There have been several potential disasters through the years. On December 14, 1987, a tornado just missed a stadium with 9,000 people in West Memphis, Arkansas, most of whom never realized a tornado had passed. On May 11 (that infamous day) in 1985, a potentially tornadic storm passed right over (Kansas City) Royals Stadium, filled with spectators. Lightning storms have passed over stadiums time and again with fans, seated on metal benches, blissfully unaware of their perilous position.

Some cities in Tornado Alley have been so fortunate, citizens have created rationales for their luck. For example, some residents of Topeka believe they are protected by Burnett Mound, a small hill on the city's outskirts. But in 1966, a violent tornado passed directly over the mound and tore through the city, killing 16 and injuring 400. Amarillo, located in the heart of the Alley, has experienced only a few tornadoes. Many residents feel that some geographical, climatological or spiritual

factor protects the city. Oklahoma City is located in one of the most potentially dangerous locations within the Alley. It has been struck by twisters at least 33 times in the past 90 years, although no major tornado has struck—yet.

Even though Tornado Alley covers a vast area, the actual chaseable terrain encompasses around 250,000 square miles, which is less than 50 percent of the total area. What limits the chaser from covering the entire area is that a large portion of the Alley consists of densely foliated and hilly terrain. The lack of visibility and inability to spot severe storms in such regions is not only frustrating, it's dangerous. This also partially accounts for the deadly history of this area.

My few ventures into the wooded country of Arkansas and Missouri were nerve-wracking and perilous. In fact, we almost contributed to the area's deadly history—for another reason. While chasing in the wooded hill country of eastern Oklahoma, Joel Ewing, a friend and fellow chaser, and I got into a shouting match over which direction we should pursue a tree-shrouded storm. We came just short of fisticuffs. On reflection, I made out well. Joel is a solid 6-foot 4-inches. I could well have wound up a piece of flying debris myself.

As a rule, I will not chase storms east of The Great Wall of Chasing, also known as Interstate 35. It runs from east-central Texas, northward through central Oklahoma and Kansas. For the most part, Interstate 35 divides the trees, to the east,

above: A vast unobstructed horizon in Tornado Alley

right: A tornado is seen forming near Miami, Texas. May 29, 1994.

from the flat farm country and plains toward the west, where the horizon and skies can merge into one hazy line. The tops of storms can be seen for well over 150 miles. It is within this "hot zone," stretching from eastern New Mexico into west Texas, Oklahoma, Kansas, eastern Colorado and southern Nebraska, that roads and visibility have created a chaser's paradise.

With such a vast area of potential chasing, there is little or no room for error in forecasting or picking the right storm. "There is a sort of built-in penalty function in storm chasing," Alan Moller, a NWS meteorologist and respected chaser, once said. "If you make a bad forecast, you go to an area that's void of storms, and you pay for it" (through lost time, money, and chances). Many times during early chases, I had been lured to far away places by what appeared to be an infallible forecast, only to watch a cloudless blue sky fade as the sun peacefully went below the skyline. The punishment of watching ordinary days, weeks, or even years of normal-climate days is enough to weed out many would-be chasers.

I may have goofed on occasion, but it only whetted my chase appetite more. Like someone once said, "One of the spices of life is to have something you desire continuously elude you."

My mission in life was still unwavering: find a tornado and capture it on film!

The base of a supercell storm exhibiting signs of rotation. West Texas.

Big Game

It sounds like a nearby waterfall.

The tornado is less than a mile away and I can hear its voice clearly. Tom brings the car to an abrupt halt, points his camera out the window and fires away. "Wait for me," I yell. I get out and run across the highway in the direction of a farmstead.

Tom's voice blares over the radio: "Warren, get the hell back! I've got to go get some more film!" I try to reach Tom with my hand-held radio, but he can't hear me over the howling wind. The snaky gray twister grows bigger and forms a large dust bowl near its base. Tom speeds down the road, still calling over the radio until his voice fades into static.

I ran up a gravel road that leads to the

A low-precipitation supercell in west Texas

farm house. It's a charming house, with a white picket fence and a swing on the front porch. It's surrounded by a flowing sea of green wheat fields.

I bang twice on the door. It is opened by a beautiful, light-haired woman wearing a white sun dress. Her eyes are the same color as the fields. I seem to know her. She smiles, reaches out, and takes my hand. Turning around, I point to the approaching tornado, which is drawing dangerously close. She leads me inside. The interior is empty except for a few pieces of antique furniture.

In the middle of the hallway, she reaches down to the wood plank floor and opens a trap door. I follow her down a flight of stairs. The basement is dark except for a few rays of light seeping in through cracks in the ceiling. At the bottom of the stairs, she turns toward me, smiling once again. Her face is lit by a single beam of light and her eyes shine like emeralds.

Suddenly, the room starts to shake. The sound of cracking wood fills the room, and dust falls from the ceiling. Debris shoots through the walls like bullets. I reach for her, the room is flooded with bright light as the roof spins away. Then, a pounding roar.

I open my eyes. For a brief moment I cower, fearing the tornado.

My dream was abruptly ended by a UPS delivery man pounding on the door. Over the last 18 hours, I had been in and out of sleep as I recovered from a serious bout of food poisoning, after eating a cold turkey sandwich from a fast food joint. Such are the hazards of storm chasing.

High Risk!

Chase Log: April 26, 1991. South-central Oklahoma.

"I hear the voice of rage and ruin." The steering wheel was my drum, and I was singing along to Creedence Clearwater Revival's "Bad Moon Rising," on some distant AM station. I was on Highway 281, just outside Apache, Oklahoma, happy to hear the chaser's anthem. Today was a "high-risk" tornado day.

My fifth tornado chase season was underway, and "the big one" had still eluded me. I was anxious to get going. Instead of hitting the road in May, as planned, I gambled and started early. April storms can be difficult to chase, because jet stream winds often move them along at 40 mph or faster. As a result, interception would be a combination of perfect timing, positioning and fortune.

I flew into Lubbock on April 21, rented a car and chased about west Texas and Oklahoma. No luck. I stopped at the NWS office near Lubbock airport to check the forecast. The weather gods were smiling on me.

The NWS 48-hour forecast model and its satellite imagery showed an impressive cyclone approaching from the west. The spiraling, comma-shaped cloud pattern over the western U.S. was a hint of trouble. I sought out a senior forecaster who happened to be an experienced chaser. "This system is incredibly dynamic," he said. "If it holds together and taps into the gulf moisture, Friday will be a big-time chase day." A chaser in Oklahoma put it more succinctly: "People are going to die on the 26th." That comment made my skin crawl. It was more than enough to keep me in the Alley for a couple of extra days, as well.

I was passing through Childress, Texas, on the morning of the 26th, en route to Wichita Falls, Texas, when I decided to stop at the NWS office and check on the latest forecast. The witch's brew of low pressure, moisture, and a strong jet stream overhead were going to produce violent weather, forecasters believed. I examined the charts and data printouts posted on a bulletin board. A forecaster handed me a printout. "You'll want to take a look at this," he said.

> "It is emphasized that this is a potentially dangerous weather situation for much of Oklahoma. Extreme instability and the expected winds aloft indicate the potential for a significant severe weather outbreak later this afternoon including the possibility of very destructive tornadoes. Residents are urged to take this situation seriously."

I read the printout twice and studied my own data. I made my way to the door and thanked the man. "Where are you heading?" he asked.

"Somewhere from west-central Oklahoma into Kansas. I'll concentrate on the dryline," I said. The dryline is the boundary, often unstable, between moist and dry air masses.

"It [the dryline] looks like a good place to start," he responded, glancing at his computer console. "I think we're out of danger here, but it sure as heck looks like a bull's eye this afternoon somewhere near the Kansas and Oklahoma border. You better be real careful today," he added.

"Well, that's what I'm here for," I said. It was hard to conceal my excitement. After four years of tornado chasing, it looked like my meteorological ship was coming in. Nothing like a terribly ominous forecast to boost the spirits.

I made my way north from Wichita Falls along Interstate 44 toward Oklahoma. I would continue north on Highway 281 towards Enid, Oklahoma, where I expected the first storms to develop near the dryline. The first growing storm clouds, or "towers," were visible in the distant west as I approached Fairview, Oklahoma. I followed them for several miles, hoping they would grow into my dream storm.

As impressive as they were, however, they abruptly collapsed into an overcast haze. Soon, other storms went up and suffered a similar fate. Something was seriously wrong with the atmosphere, I thought. In an hour or so, the sky above me was covered with a thick deck of gray, stratus clouds. I pulled to the side of the road and got out. I studied my road map and began to plan my southern return route to Lubbock.

I was about to give up and go back, but a glance over my shoulder convinced me otherwise. It was about 3:30 p.m. and what I saw stunned me. Up through the ugly cloud bank towards the east, a mass of ivory-white storm clouds were shooting up through the sky in the typical A-bomb style. "Holy mother of nature! That's it!" I yelled, as I turned the car around and raced east along Highway 60 toward Enid.

The eastern sky soon revealed a tremendous storm with a rounded anvil-like head. From the base of the storm upward, the clouds were twisted, like a barber's pole. The storm was rotating.

Just west of Enid, I picked up a radio station in the midst of transmitting a tornado warning: "Take shelter immediately. A tornado is reported on the ground just east of Enid," it said. I glanced at the gas gauge—empty. I made the mistake of not keeping my gas tank full. I cursed and pulled into the first gas station I saw. I ran inside, rudely passed two people standing in line, tossed the clerk a $10 bill,

Expanding A-bomb style clouds indicate that a highly unstable atmosphere is preparing to generate severe weather.

raced back to the car, pumped and tore off down the highway after my storm. I had wasted precious, precious time.

East of Enid, along Highway 64, the sides of the road were lined with cars. It seemed that everyone was pointing or staring at the storm. Moments later, I saw why.

Protruding from the clouds, hovering over green fields some five miles away, was a long rope-like funnel snaking its way down from the dark base of the cloud. I pulled to the side of the highway. Simultaneously, the funnel completely vanished. I continued traveling east, guessing that the small twister was but a hint that bigger things were coming.

I tracked the storm bouncing between a maze of dusty dirt roads and the highway. I kept as close as possible to the updraft base, the area where a tornado usually drops. I pulled over, again, when I noticed the entire base of the storm was beginning to rapidly rotate and contract.

Swirling storm clouds cross the road.

Suddenly, a large, white, cone-shaped funnel developed from a "wall cloud" in the center of the updraft. In a minute, the cone transformed into an enormous wedge-shaped tornado that spread out over the field and began ripping up dirt, plants, shrubs and anything in its path, throwing the material up and away from the vortex.

After I came to my senses—after all, this was the first time I had seen such a sight—I jumped back into the car and tore after the wedge. I found that the storm was moving away at better than 40 mph. I drove as fast as I could down the dirt road, video camera in one hand, steering wheel in the other. My challenge was to keep the tornado framed in the center of the viewfinder. I was completely overwhelmed. "This is a big, big … Yes, folks, it's a mile-wide Oklahoma twister!" I narrated into the microphone. Eventually, I calmed down and shut my mouth. The wind did a better job of describing the storm.

I was able to drive parallel with the tornado for several miles, keeping an eye on it to avoid becoming one more piece of flying debris. I should have heard faint echoes of mothers telling their kids to "avoid that Faidley kid."

So massive and so fast was the tornado that I couldn't tell for sure which way it was heading. Illusion was also a risk here. Since my mind had never encountered this type of image, it did not register as "the real thing." I wanted to get the best pictures ever taken of a tornado; I didn't want to become this tornado's playmate on a dirt road with no escape.

I reached Highway 15 and sped north, directly toward the tornado. It appeared to be five miles away. I kept the video camera focused on the vortex, which became ominously larger as I closed in. It looked more like a huge plume of smoke than a mile-wide tornado.

A radio weatherman examining the radar screen did everything he could to stress the danger: "Folks," he said, "please believe me. These storms are killing people as I talk. The radar signatures are from another world. Please take shelter if you are in the path of these dangerous storms."

The landscape quickly dropped down into a river area, thickly lined with trees, which completely cut off my view of the twister. I approached a metal span bridge and noticed the tops of the trees beginning to bend in the direction of the tornado. I was unsure of the tornado's location, and I locked up the brakes just before the bridge. The car spun around on the highway shoulder, and I started back south until I could once again see the tornado over the trees. Then, a quarter mile from where I stood, the tornado crossed the road.

I turned around again and headed back north. Debris was falling from the sky on the far side of the bridge. Not wanting to get whacked by a stray two-by-four, I pulled over and narrated the closing events as the twister churned onward and disappeared into the rain. I anxiously examined my road maps and tried to find an eastward route. It was useless. The nearest highway going east was too far. Several other people went zooming by, trying to catch the shadowy twister. It was long gone.

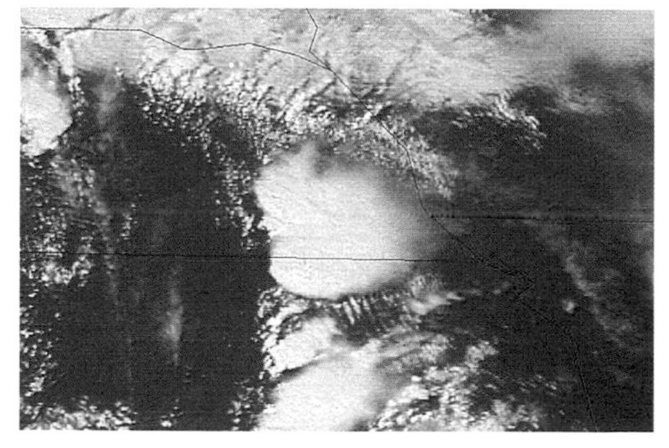

top left: Faidley's first confirmed tornado, captured on video tape. NE of Enid, Oklahoma. April 26, 1991.

top right: Faidley with towering storm clouds moving in

left: Satellite image of supercell cloud tops seen over the Kansas and Nebraska region as they produce deadly twisters

I sighed. The chase was over and I could put a notch in my belt. I had my first tornado!

I sat roadside and watched the mother supercell, which spawned the tornado, move swiftly away, still harboring the vortex within the rain shafts. I recalled the words of Joel Ewing, who said pursuing tornadoes was the "ultimate big-game hunt." After years of work and tens of thousands of miles of hunting, man, was he right!

While I was out shooting, Howard Bluestein, the NSSL scientist, was a few miles away taking readings of the tornado on an experimental Doppler unit. His measurement—270 to 287 mph—was the highest tornadic winds recorded.

I stopped that night in Elk City, Oklahoma, after fatigue and storm-overload set in. Television stations and cable networks were broadcasting live coverage of the day's events. I discovered that my storm was only one of a series of supercells that produced violent tornadoes, including at least one killer tornado near Wichita. One news station showed footage taken by a Wichita news crew. It was remarkable video, which showed them outrunning a tornado in their car—then seeking shelter in an underpass as the tornado roared by. Despite my exhaustion, I had to see my own footage. I hooked my video camera to the television and watched. It was all right but nothing prize-winning. The tornado I taped was so large, it looked more like a smoke plume. My insecurity increased as I realized I had shot only a few stills.

No sooner did my head hit the pillow than I lapsed into an uneasy sleep complete with tornado nightmares. Among the most vivid: I'm attending a football game, and I, alone, see a twister approaching. The roar of the crowd soon mixes with the roar of the twister. People try to squeeze under seats or run to exits, others are picked up by the funnel, the blimp is punctured by debris, and it spirals out of control. In another dream, I watch as a tornado hits a fleet of military bombers, and they become a glowing, radioactive vortex. I slept until almost noon on the 27th and headed back to Lubbock.

As I drove towards Lubbock, radio news reports provided updated information about the outbreak. More than 50 tornadoes had occurred over a six-state area. Twenty-one people had been killed. One tornado, packing winds estimated at over

260 mph, hit Andover, Kansas, obliterating a mobile home park, killing 13. A warning had been issued 20 minutes before the tornado struck. My radioactive dream almost came to life—so to speak—when a reporter noted that the Wichita twister had just missed hitting sixteen B-1B bombers (which could have been loaded with nuclear weapons) at McConnell Air Force Base.

Several months after the outbreak, stories of actual bizarre events began to surface. A woman working at a greenhouse near Wichita reported that the tornado turned "pink" after it hit a section of geraniums. One man was impaled by a two-by-four that was driven into his side, exiting near his groin. The board missed his vital organs, and after fifteen days in the hospital he went home. A video camera mounted in a police car captured shocking footage of the Andover tornado as it bore down upon the trailer park. The goose bump-generating footage showed people casually conducting everyday business, like walking the dog, as the twister approached.

Who's Been Sleeping in My Bed?

The greatest worries of a chaser, after the day's work is over, center around the stomach and lodging. This is where prayer and good networking come in handy, for eating in last-resort restaurants can be as risky as chasing a tornado.

I have been fortunate considering the range of places in which I have downed a meal. Many restaurants in the Plains push a fare of heavy, grease-laden meals. Convenience stores have heat-lamped glass display cases filled with soggy hamburgers, greasy chicken and the ever popular deep-fried okra and potato wedges. One chaser resorted to cooking frozen dinners on his engine block in an effort to expand his culinary options. Others have wisely chosen to sacrifice valuable trunk space, and in lieu of chase equipment, carry an ice chest filled with healthier food.

That's not to say that chaseland cuisine is to be completely avoided. Tom and I once drove 100 miles out of the way on a bust chase day just to eat a barbecued roast beef sandwich in Dickens, Texas. It seems there's a kind of barbecue war going on there. The battle has produced a sauce that is beyond mouthwatering, and it has become a ritual for us to stop there at least once a year.

The golden rule of lodging is to inspect one's bedding before tucking oneself in. Chasers share nightmares about what they have found crawling, residing in or sticking to their sheets. Mattresses range from wet-sponge status to petrified. Carpets and shower stalls in many motels are worthy of advanced scientific research. One of my more intriguing moments came at an Oklahoma motel where, in a matter of seconds, I watched the water turn from crystal-clear to coffee-brown.

Sometimes, you can't be picky. In the last two weeks of May and first week of June, I have become accustomed to competing for rooms with cowboys, hunters, religious groups and softball teams.

Success and Outlaws

My storm chasing evolved into professional, detailed adventures as spring of 1992 approached. Now, storm chasing involved a wealth of camera, video, computer and support equipment, months of preparation and thousands of dollars in expenses. Laptop computers, satellite links, cellular phones, high-tech video and motion picture cameras put a quick end to tape recorders, pay phones and note pads.

Weatherstock, in four years, had thrived. I had signed contracts with 11 foreign photographic agents who marketed my still images and motion picture film worldwide. In the span of three years, I produced eight 1-hour videos on the subject of severe weather. I even patented a device which holds a video camera to a car's interior windshield.

Sign in a Kansas motel room

The media frenzy that I had seen so often when I covered news events now focused on this odd storm chaser from Tucson. Radio and television talk shows flew me (and my clips) across the country. Reporters from Tucson to Tokyo sought my story. Magazines and tabloids billed me as the "Cyclone Cowboy," "Lightning Stalker," the "Fearless Weatherman," "Flash Faidley," and the "Tornado Man."

Wackos provided me with entertainment that I couldn't have found elsewhere. One swore that he had invented a "tornado-killing machine." If I would get him near a tornado, he pledged, "I'll zap it for you." Another weird call came from a man who claimed to have worked at the top secret "Area 51" in Nevada as a "government public relations agent." He woke me up at 4:30 one morning after reading a feature in the *Los Angeles Times.* I must be warned, he pleaded, that "Flying saucers were causing lightning storms in New Mexico" and that "I should let them work in peace." "Yes, I'll be extra careful to avoid them if I ever film there," I promised, reminiscing about my Don Quixote windmill experience near Sonoita.

It was also during this period that the concept of "chasing storms" became trendy.

In 1977, when veteran chaser Dave Hoadley published his first edition of *Stormtrack*, he wrote: "One of my long-standing concerns has been that storm chasers may eventually draw too much publicity, and chasing will become another mass cult of the leisure class, much as scuba diving or hang gliding."

Dave's fears materialized in the early 1980s as the ranks of part-time, hobbyist chasers increased each chase season. This growth was fueled by the mass media. First, chasers were receiving increasing coverage; moreover, more time was being devoted on television to the weather events themselves. News stations in Tornado Alley aggressively chased storms in "live weather" vans, and the public's exposure to severe weather changed. Graphic, live video replaced outdated newsreels; modern radar systems pin-pointed storm cells on television sets. The competition to get the best storm footage even motivated a few stations to hire seasoned chasers and spotters to intercept storms for their news and weather reports.

But it was the advent of affordable home video cameras that finally propelled chasing into a thrill-seeking pastime. Suddenly, anyone had the means of capturing stunning, live weather on video tape and be the hero of the 10 o'clock news or make a few bucks. The hideous Andover, Kansas, tornado of April 1991, became the country's most pictorially documented tornadic event of all time. Several amateur videographers in Wichita captured the now-classic footage of the tornado as it swept through the Golden Spur Mobile Home Park. One chaser had to retain a lawyer to handle the legal problems surrounding the usage of his footage.

Now, routinely, a severe weather watch is a signal for hundreds of people to grab a video camera and head for the Great Plains, or elsewhere. A Kansas man, his wife and infant son, drove off in pursuit of a tornado after seeing a live radar display on television. Unfortunately, the wind tipped over his truck. In May 1991, a Spearman, Texas man taped a tornado as it approached his home. Soon, his neigh-

Storm chasers speed by, heading towards a storm.

bor's home disintegrated piece by piece. The man was nearly fried by a lightning bolt, but he continued taping, and narrating, until he was hit by flying debris.

Like a Sunday matinee, a storm on a weekend attracts an additional audience. Roadsides were so crowded during one weekend storm near Oklahoma City that neither emergency vehicles nor bona fide spotters could park. "If you could predict when and where a tornado would hit a trailer park," said one veteran chaser, "you could sell thousands of tickets and refreshments."

But despite the numerous risks, not a single person is known to have been killed while actively engaged in a chase. People have been killed in autos returning from so-called chases, authorities say. One chaser hit a black cow standing in the middle of a dark asphalt highway. (This is why many chasers now use the brightest head lamps they can find.) With everyone and his uncle (and even some aunts) chasing storms, it's only a matter of time before nature deals someone a fatal blow.

Trouble on the Way

One of the many hazards on the road, flash flooding

A handful of the television-and tragedy-inspired chasers became so infatuated with tornadoes, that they extended their chase scope beyond their hometowns. A few devised clever ways to legitimize themselves, claiming to be official storm spotters or researchers. Unlike the majority of people who chase or spot storms, these "outlaw" chasers have no interest in meteorology, and they have little respect for the dangers and consequences of bad weather.

Legitimate chasers and spotters began to suffer the wrath of the outlaws. During a tornado outbreak in southwest Kansas, several carloads of outlaws used a farmer's field as a shortcut and nearly caused a serious automobile accident on the main highway. The sheriff went so far as to notify all chasers that they had to "call in" before chasing and receive permission—or risk jail. The well has been poisoned to such an extent that a Texas legislator proposed an "anti-chase" law. Several National Weather Service offices closed their doors to all chasers and spotters.

Despite the growing pains associated with the sudden popularity of chasing, my conversion from nomadic photographer to a professional storm chaser was a success. I could afford to chase full-time, almost anytime, any way, and anywhere I wanted.

But before I could return to the Alley and seek out more twisters, I had to challenge yet another kind of beast.

When the Devil Screams

Chase Log: August 22, 1992.
Miami, Florida

I hit the corridors of the Miami airport at a near run, fighting to keep two large shoulder bags from throwing me off balance. Not only was I late for a 10 p.m. rendezvous at the National Hurricane Center, but I also suspected the rental car counter would be in its customary pre-storm frenzy as people departed—or, in the case of journalists like myself, invaded—Ground Zero.

Andrew, the first named storm of the year in the Atlantic Ocean, was not expected to make landfall for two more days, if at all. The storm, at this point, was a minor concern mentioned with a casual smile. During the long flight from Tucson, I overheard more than one person joke about having a hurricane

Photograph of Hurricane Andrew used on the cover of Life *Magazine. August 1992.*

party, or comment about the possibility of missing a golf date. One businessman, consuming gin at least as fast as the jet did fuel, was offering a wacky theory that hurricanes could not hit Florida "because of a shielding power" generated by the so-called "greenhouse effect." The storm was the "most dangerous of all time," said a passenger who boarded in Houston. I avoided becoming entangled in the conversation.

I rounded the last corner of the corridor leading to the rental counters, slowing my pace to avoid alerting the clerk that an excited chase journalist was there to pick up his chase vehicle. ("Yes, I'd like the car that best resists wind. By the way, does it float?") The rental counter was not busy.

"Would you like the loss and damage waiver," the clerk asked.

"Oh … I don't really think I'll need it … Well, what the heck, why don't you go ahead and include it *this* time," I told her. I got my car and headed down Highway 1 toward the National Hurricane Center (NHC).

Located on the sixth floor of the tallest building in Coral Gables, the NHC is a war room, complete with emergency back-up systems and steel window shutters designed to repel any storm.* This would be my first visit to the Center; I was nervous, but took comfort in knowing that I would soon be in my element (so to speak).

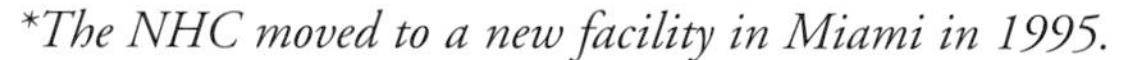
**The NHC moved to a new facility in Miami in 1995.*

The doors opened, and the silence was broken by a furor of sound and activity. People were hustling through corridors carrying equipment or papers. The space was cast in an artificial glow created by the lights of news crews. I followed a variety of colored cables to the main forecast room. I had the distinct feeling I was on the set of a disaster movie.

The forecast area overflowed with reporters, meteorologists and a handful of chasers. A large monitor showed a continuous color satellite loop. That was Andrew. I watched for a moment, reassuring myself the storm was still on its way. Robert Sheets, director of the NHC, was being interviewed by a television reporter. "Andrew is the storm we have long feared in south Florida," the reporter concluded. In the middle of the room was the nerve center—a circle of computers and monitors manned by forecasters reading and updating data from remote stations and hurricane-tracking aircraft.

I stood against a wall, out of the way, and simply took in the moment. To kill time, I took a few shots of the monitor showing Andrew swirling in the background. I surveyed the crowd and found my contacts, veteran hurricane chasers Mike Laca and Steve Wachholder. Our common interest in tropical weather had kept us exchanging information and videos over the years, but this was our first meeting. Both of them had extensive experience chasing hurricanes and tropical storms. We quickly turned to the business at hand: how to pursue Andrew—and stay alive doing it.

Andrew had the potential to become an extremely dangerous hurricane, according to Mike. "Well, Warren, you made the right decision," he said, remembering my doubtful tone in our last conversation. "Looks like Andrew will maintain its course and hit us in just over twenty-four hours." I could sense the excitement in his voice. "Steve and I just studied the latest data, and it's about 520 miles from Miami. It's heading in our direction at around 14 miles per hour."

"What's the latest wind measurement?" I asked. "Sustained at 110 miles per hour, but you know they're probably higher," he said. Steve said forecasters

left: The National Hurricane Center in Coral Gables, Florida, August 1992.

thought the forward speed might increase to 20 mph by Sunday morning. We agreed to meet again at noon Sunday to analyze data and scout for an intercept location.

I made the mistake of not reserving a motel room, so I had to drive to North Miami to find a room. I wasted no time showering and diving into bed. But I couldn't fall asleep despite my fatigue. My mind conjured all sorts of scenarios. I envisioned flood waters and how I would escape. What would I do with my camera gear? What should my settings be, and what would I do if equipment failed? I had awaited this moment for years, and I didn't want to blow it. I would fail as a photojournalist if I didn't capture Andrew. Pictures of hurricanes in daylight and "in progress" were extremely rare and were among the most in demand. I tried to think of matters besides this hurricane. My thoughts drifted back to the Atlantic.

Andrew would hit early Monday if it maintained its forward speed and direction, allowing me to shoot it in subdued daylight. If it came sooner, I'd be shooting in darkness. All recent U.S. hurricanes had hit at night.

A news announcer's voice awoke me on Sunday. They had turned up the volume in an adjacent room, and I tuned in. "Some gas stations are reporting small lines, but I don't think that you'll have any trouble working your way inland this morning," a reporter said. I jumped up, took my habitual glance out the window, squinted at a crystal-clear sky, packed my bags and went on my way.

Small lines were indeed beginning to form at gas stations on Highway 1, and traffic heading out of town was increasing. I stopped at the first convenience store to buy items on my checklist labeled "pre-hurricane, at the scene items." This included two gallons of bottled water, a small food supply. (Snickers bars, beef jerky, Cokes, some bananas and a box of Pop-Tarts), two cans of tire fixer, a road flare and a couple of small candles. Several people waiting at the counter saw my supplies and went back for the same items. I filled the car's gas tank as the line to the station grew.

With an hour to kill, I decided it was time for a hot meal. Those are in short supply during storm chases. I grabbed a copy of the Sunday *Miami Herald* with the bold headline "Bigger, Stronger, Closer." Andrew was the only topic at breakfast.

One frail man, in his 60s, was arguing with other diners: "I have been through a few of them," the man said. "As long as you're not too close to the water, it's no big deal." A woman sitting in a booth across from the man immediately jumped into the conversation. She was "getting the hell out of town," because she went through Hurricane Betsy. That hurricane, which struck south Florida in 1965, had killed 13 people.

I wanted only to avoid the subject of foul weather. No chance. At the moment my food arrived, a woman noticed my company shirt, which has a logo containing a lightning bolt, tornado and the symbol for a hurricane. Her eyes grew, and I was bombarded with the usual questions: "Are you here for the hurricane? Why do you do it? How do you earn a living? Are you afraid?" My food got to my mouth colder than I would have liked.

Gas stations now had lines extending well onto the highway, and convenience store parking lots were filled. I pulled into one store to shoot the buying frenzy, only to discover that the shelves had been swept clean of anything for storm survival, including bottled water and batteries. A few people complained about the shortage, but a heavy-set, red-faced lady shouted, "You should save some things for this kind of emergency."

Entrepreneurs sprung into action. One man, with a sign reading "Andrew's Last Chance Market," set up a small emergency supply center on the side of the road, where he hawked candles, batteries and jugs of water. Up and down the highway, businessmen and residents boarded up windows and moved items like shopping carts that could become flying missiles.

The midday scene at the NHC was again a beehive of activity. I spotted Steve and Mike near the large monitor, and they brought me up-to-date. Overnight, Andrew had been classified "an extremely dangerous" category 4 hurricane and was churning the ocean east of the Bahamas. A category 4 hurricane (on an intensity rating scale of 1 to 5) has sustained winds near the surface of 131 to 155 mph and storm surges of 13 to 18 feet. Satellite images clearly showed the eye wall, the center of the storm, expanding and contracting. This was a sign that the storm was maintaining its intensity. It was also becoming evident that Andrew's ferocious path was likely to remain constant, taking the storm directly into south Florida. I knew its enormous potential, for I had overheard forecasters speculating, to themselves, about the best way to avoid outright panic. Andrew, they said, would likely be one of the most powerful hurricanes ever to hit the U.S.—if not the most.

How would we pursue Andrew? Our goal was to position ourselves where the passage of the eye—some 10 to 20 miles in circumference—was most likely to occur.

Mike and I decided to scout the coastal areas and find a suitable location to ride out the storm. Any such building or structure would have to offer complete protection from flying debris and a storm surge of more than 15 feet high.

I paid for a hotel room in Coral Gables at the Howard Johnson, near the NHC. I filled the sink with water, expecting the water to be shut off when the storm hit.

Fort Andrew

We hunted for our perch for several hours and finally agreed on a seven-story parking garage in Coconut Grove, five miles southwest of the NHC. This sturdy parking lot was a thick-walled, concrete fortress. The exterior walls were lined with square openings that offered wonderful vantage points. It also offered us a (vital) 360-degree view. The only blockage was to the east, where a 21-story office building blocked our view of a private marina and Biscayne Bay.

I was worried initially about the blockage, but it was just as well, for the building might actually shield us from boat parts and other debris. Our

"Ft. Andrew"

fortress, which I dubbed "Fort Andrew," stood on land higher than the marina. Flood waters would only reach the lower floors, I figured. Moreover, Key Biscayne, to the east, would serve as a wave blocker, subduing any massive wind-driven surge. I had never been happier to occupy an upper floor of a parking garage.

The remainder of the day was spent walking about the area, examining nearby buildings, exits and possible escape routes. It was an exceptionally tranquil afternoon, and I walked about enjoying what generations of humankind know as "the calm before the storm." But other telltale details belied the quiet day. The marina was deserted. Wispy, high cirrus clouds marked the edge of Andrew's crown. And two small, red and black hurricane flags flew from the marina's mast. How many mariners from how many centuries, I wondered, had left on such beautiful pre-storm days, never to re-appear?

The docks were crammed with everything from small sailboats to exquisite yachts. Many were tied to docks with the heaviest rope I have seen. I overheard one boat owner tell a younger worker, "Tying the boats to the dock would destroy both the boats and the docks." The safest thing was to "sink the damned boats," he said. The worker replied sharply, "Well, if people would have moved their boats inland, or further up north, we wouldn't have this problem." I took several photographs of the docks and boats, noting my exact position, expecting to return for aftermath images. A handful of workers in the marina's commercial area labored feverishly to finish placing metal and plywood panels over plate-glass windows.

The sun retreated, and I returned to Fort Andrew to make yet another final equipment check. I examined and re-examined cameras, lenses, flash units, rope, rescue strobe, safety glasses, waterproof bags and more. Mike and Steve razzed me about the equipment dangling from every part of me. "Don't laugh," I told them, "It'll serve its purpose before the night's over."

Steve and Mike established a fifth floor "command center," complete with radios, television and a pile of camera and electronic gear. A handful of people living in the surrounding neighborhoods drove to the garage to drop off their cars en route to safer surroundings. We were, admittedly, a strange sight, and they asked us what we planned to do. Watch the storm, we said. Most seemed amused but happier yet that someone would be keeping an eye on their cars.

Mike and Steve studied the latest data from radio and television. I went to the top of the garage and took the first watch. The Miami skyline, off to the north, was beautiful. Below, I watched a group of kittens frolic in a yard.

Steve joined me. We pondered what the night would bring and what we should do in specific circumstances. My greatest worry was flying debris, even though I had a 21-story shield partially in front of me. What would we do in the event of a storm surge? (Had we been too optimistic parking our own cars on the fourth floor?) I was worried about getting our cars out after the storm. We implemented a buddy system to keep from becoming separated.

We watched live news coverage on television to entertain and inform ourselves. An electric company spokesperson said power would be left on until it was knocked out. A Coast Guard official gave a chilling report of a boat somewhere out in the Atlantic calling desperately for help after getting caught in gigantic swells. "There's nothing that we can do," he solemnly noted.

I returned to my car, laid back, closed my eyes, and discovered there was no way to relax. A gust of wind would rock the car or a sudden thought about my equipment would pop into my mind. I almost fell asleep once, but a loudspeaker mounted on a police car, giving a final evacuation notice, kept me awake.

We took turns, like sentries, scanning the horizon. By 11:00 p.m. there was still no sign of Andrew, except an occasional gust. Maybe the hurricane had stalled or turned away from our location. But the updates on radio and TV said Andrew was making a beeline inland—directly for us.

Hell's Symphony

At about 2:30 a.m., it was clear this would be no ordinary night.

Winds had been increasing all night, and in the not-distant northeast, bright aquamarine flashes filled the horizon as power lines began to arc and explode. The eerie glows were reminiscent of the Gulf War coverage on television. "Better get up here real quick," I yelled to Steve and Mike who were still watching the television on the level below. "There's a hell of a light show on its way!"

No sooner had Mike and Steve reached me when a powerful gale slammed into the garage. The air was immediately filled with a cracking whip sound as high-tension electrical lines began to collide and arc. Mike ran to the west side of the garage and began videotaping the bright blue electrical explosions. "Watch those loose wires," I yelled. "They'll cut your head off!"

Steve and I attempted to measure the wind speeds with a small hand-held anemometer. Leaning halfway out the side of the fourth floor opening, in a rather awkward position, Steve steadied the meter with two hands while I pointed a flash-light at the dial and called out the readings. "Fifty-five," I shouted, as the needle on the meter swung back and forth. "Steve, are you sure this thing is accurate?" I asked. "Hell, yes," he replied. A stronger wind hit, and the needle hit 65 mph. "That's it," Steve shouted. "It's too dangerous; I can't hold on!" The increasing winds and rain began to swirl through the garage.

The passage of each new squall made the storm more potent. As the winds increased, so did the decibel level. Sparking electrical lines were the first sounds we heard, but as the moments passed, they were joined by the rattles of metal trash cans rolling down the street. Sounds, a phenomenon I really hadn't taken into account, changed in frequency and intensity. A symphony of nature and debris were warming up for a concert of annihilation!

By 3:45 a.m., new sounds filled the darkened interior of the garage. Breaking glass, as windows imploded from the force of the wind or were hit by flying debris. Then delicate wind chime sounds as glass blew down the street. In the garage, we were serenaded by the constant blasts of car alarms that had been activated by the wind or debris. But soon, all these sounds were muffled by the low-pitched roar of a hurricane.

Mike and Steve concentrated their taping on the east and south sides of the garage as winds, now blowing steadily at about 100 mph, began to tear things apart. Steve had a powerful hand-held spotlight that he used as a video light. I volunteered

to hold the light, as they filmed the wind shredding a palm tree's fronds. It was too dark to take any still images. I worried that Andrew's force might diminish by daybreak. "Don't worry, Warren, it will still be blasting away when the sun comes up," Mike assured me. I felt like a child who had been assured that his toys would still be in his room when he awoke.

Despite Mike's assurances, and my own calculations, I made the decision to leave the safe confines of Fort Andrew. With a powerful flash, I'd be able to shoot some images of the mayhem on the street. This was risky, I knew, but if I could walk alongside the garage, using it as a wind break, I'd be able to venture out from time to time and get a good shot.

We used the garage's main elevator until the main body of the storm hit. Once the power was threatened, we decided to avoid it. ("Whiz-boy photographer spends entire hurricane trapped in elevator," I imagined the headline would read. Or worse, "Skeletons of storm chasers found on Level III. They should have stayed away from the Faidley boy!")

Shredded palms after Hurricane Andrew

Several large plate-glass windows near the garage's stairwells had been blown out. One window remained but was severely fractured. I moved by this window with great caution, as it pulsated in and out from the pressure of the winds. I knew that it too would soon implode. I reached gingerly to open the heavy metal door to the stairwell and prepared to jump quickly back. Heavy metal doors can open or close with explosive power from wind pressure within the stairwell. Earlier, I had turned the knob to a lower floor door, and it swung open violently, crashing against the concrete wall, with the force to pulverize an arm or a head.

Inside the stairwell, I had the sensation I was within the bowels of a sinking ship. The chamber was lit by a weird yellowish glow, from an emergency light that intensified and decreased with hypnotic frequency. The musty smell of salty sea water mixed with the odor of wet dust, and water poured from the concrete steps. It was sticky and warm, and despite the thick layers of concrete all around, I could still hear and feel Andrew breathing like a panting animal ready to pounce.

I walked carefully down the slick steps, keeping track of each floor. I opened the door cautiously and passed into the open. I spun around in terror and groped for the steel door, but the wind slammed it shut. A sick feeling welled inside me; I realized I had not found ground level, but a basement. In the pitch black, I reached for my flashlight. It had been partially crushed and was useless. I turned on my emergency strobe light and, between flashes, examined the door. It appeared that it could not be opened from my side.

Two immediate thoughts: I was going to miss the whole damn hurricane after all, or I was going to die like a drowned rat when this place flooded. I remembered our earlier premonitions (and headlines) in the elevator. I chose not to hunt for another way out, but instead to challenge the door. I played with the locking mechanism and, with the aid of my Swiss Army knife, partially exposed a plate necessary to open the door. I placed black photographer's tape on the door to avoid making this error again and continued my battle to get outside.

I found ground level, and I was greeted by a stiff breeze and rain. Right by the exit, I found someone lying on the sidewalk. From a safe distance and with my finger on the camera flash trigger—a flash is an excellent eye-stunning weapon—I yelled out, "Hey! Are you OK?" There was no response. "Do you know that this place could be flooded?" I shouted over the wind. I then moved in closer to see if he was alive. I heard an unintelligible mumble, then he curled up into a ball. I backed away and headed for the main opening. This street person could well be on the verge of becoming a sea person.

I rounded the corner and was hit by a wall of water and wind with a force that drove me to the ground. I started crawling toward the concrete walkway perpendicular to the garage. I lifted my camera, fired off a few frames, and ducked down behind the wall, more afraid of flying debris than the wind or rain. As I rose up again, a bright flash between me and the marina lit up the area to the east. I was certain I saw a debris-laden wall of water less than a hundred feet away, and I wasted no time sprinting back to Fort Andrew.

I turned the corner and watched a 55-gallon drum cartwheel down the road and smash into the walkway where I had stood seconds ago. I retreated to the safety of the garage walls to catch my breath and let my equipment dry. A stream of blood ran down my arm. I had no idea of the cause but assumed it was flying glass. I pulled a bandanna from my bag and tied it over the wound.

While we sat in the relative safety of the borrowed fortress, other parts of south Florida were being subjected to a brutal beating. At 4:45 a.m., the center of the hurricane's eye was about 18 miles southeast of us and about to reach land. Five minutes later, the NHC recorded a wind of 164 mph. (Then the NHC's rooftop anemometer blew apart.) Moments later, a loud thump shook the entire NHC building. The mystery noise turned out to be the 2,000-pound radar unit, which had plunged from its 10-foot tower onto the roof. In parts of

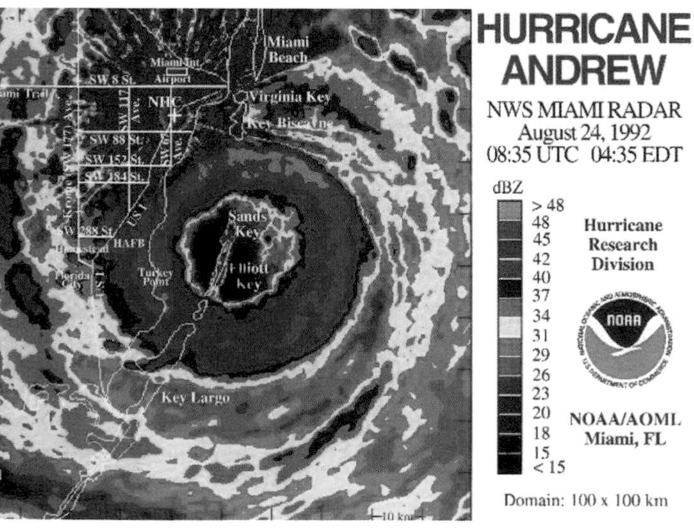

Source: NOAA / AOML / Hurricane Research Division

Homestead and Florida City, families frantically moved from room to room as their homes were slowly ripped apart by gales of 170 mph.

Steve and Mike were again filming the palm tree when I returned to the fifth floor. The tree was now but a stub with a single, pitiful frond. "Can't you guys find anything more exciting?" I asked. Steve handed me his video camera and asked me to tape him narrating. He spoke like a reporter on the 10 o'clock news. A large plate-glass window in the office building exploded with a loud pop. We scrambled for cover from shards of flying glass.

Against the shelter of a concrete wall, I suddenly remembered the storm surge.

"It looked like the ocean was filled with boats and debris, and it was only a few hundred feet from the garage!" I told them. My description was cut short when the garage rocked. Had we been hit by an earthquake? We froze, then looked up. The overhead sprinkler pipes were swaying.

Andrew churns the ocean.

The hurricane had reached its peak by 5:15 a.m., and the northern portion of the eye wall was upon us. My ears popped, a signal the air pressure had dropped suddenly. The shaking of the garage turned into a constant vibration. For the first time, I became concerned about the structural integrity of our fort. Engineers had assured me, following Hurricane Gilbert, that concrete parking garages were safe and designed to flex. Still, the jiggling garage left me on edge.

The iron sprinkler pipes, attached to the concrete ceiling with metal rods and straps, worked loose from the anchors. Several collapsed and crashed to the floor. I saw one pipe hanging by a single strap as it swung back and forth over a new Jaguar. I pulled the pipe away from the car and let it dangle to the side.

We could see through the broken windows of the office building next door. The interior rooms were swallowing up rain and winds. To the south, we watched as a home, fitted with heavy-duty shutters, was slowly picked apart. First, the winds got under the shutters and started slamming them back and forth. The windows vanished seconds later. The crack-wham of the shutters was one of the few sounds that consistently overcame the storm's wail.

The rotating winds attacked everywhere. They descended, at one point, on a grated, metal garage door at the office building's ground level. Piece by piece, the winds twisted the door from the building as if peeling the husk from a piece of corn.

I volunteered to hold the spotlight as Steve taped the bashing shutters. (At last, he had become bored with the pitiful palm tree.) A tremendous burst of wind hit the garage, and I instinctively looked to see if I was clear of the pipes. A large tree between us and the house disappeared from the spotlight. Steve was stunned. "My God, did you see that, it vanished!" he exclaimed. The gusts had to be well in excess of 140 mph. I sensed that "eddies" or vortices within the eye wall's wind flow were responsible for the greatest gusts. "Are we living through a tornado or an earthquake?" I asked Steve.

It was useless to try and walk in any area not protected from the wind. I made one feeble attempt to go to the fourth floor to check our cars, but I couldn't make it past the 15 feet of unprotected walkway. The once impressive roar fizzled to a high-pitched, jet-engine sound. Yet, now and again, a rogue howl would make my skin crawl. "The devil is screaming!" I yelled at Steve.

I looked often at my watch and the blood-soaked bandanna. I was anxious for light, which was still 90 minutes off. Steve and Mike continued their video taping, and I held the spotlight. My worst fear—not getting "the image"—was consuming me.

We had seen a security guard earlier but had assumed we were the only others in Fort Andrew. Just before sunrise, we discovered we were wrong. Out of the darkness, two wet figures appeared. The two, who owned a boat in the marina, wanted to be able to return to their boat immediately following the storm.

A Walk on the Wild Side

I detected a very faint glow in the sky about 6 a.m. Within the next half-hour, the sky gradually turned into an eerie, cobalt blue hue. It fit the mood of the mayhem. The light revealed a landscape of ruin. The surge I thought I had seen had, indeed, occurred. A 20-foot boat and the outer edge of a floating debris pile sat only a few hundred feet from the garage entrance. We had been spared the flooding but only by the narrowest of margins. The large tree we had seen vanish was rediscovered—in the side of a tractor trailer rig. The palm tree, a defiant symbol for us, was a battered stump.

The light increased to a photographable level. I donned my gear.

I surveyed the devastation from the second level and felt like a paratrooper awaiting the "go" to jump into the netherworld. My wait of five years was about to end, and nothing was going to stop me. My attack would be conducted at f/2.8 and 1/15 second. Unlike the artistic

Boat and debris near the entrance to "Ft. Andrew"

top: Marina adjacent to "Fort Andrew" before Hurricane Andrew, August 23, 1992

bottom: Marina adjacent to "Fort Andrew" after Hurricane Andrew, August 24, 1992

possibilities of tornadic and lightning storms, this was strictly a mission of gathering news images, as fast as I could, before the wind and rain subsided.

I offered a half grin over my shoulder to Mike and Steve. "Show time," I said.

Winds were still blasting away at over 100 mph. I avoided the basement and walked out. Homecoming time. The once unresponsive man lying on the ground was now shaking his fist at the sky and cursing. He was a strange sideshow to this extraordinary main event. I was once again hit by a gale as I turned the corner. Only in a crouched position, was I able to walk, step by step. I could well have auditioned for a Frankenstein movie. Lateral gusts knocked me off balance, sending me to the ground. Walking never required such physical and mental energy. Apart from the wind, I worried about debris. Not an illogical worry when you're watching unidentified objects flying overhead like cruise missiles.

I made it to the east side of the office building after a slow and careful trek in the direction of the marina. I heard a crash of glass somewhere to my side. I unwisely glanced up—then prayed that remains of shattered windows didn't fall to the ground and put an end to my career. I fired off a few frames with my waterproof 35mm camera. Suddenly, a powerful burst of wind grabbed the large waterproof bag on my back and spun me around, pushing me down the stairs and toward the boiling storm surge. One step from the water, I reached out and clutched a piece of the brass railing. Even that was too late. Half my body and my gear bag plunged into the water. I pulled myself out of the water and crawled back onto the steps, soaking wet, with a throbbing forearm. I gathered my wits, determined that my arm wasn't broken and decided—a little late—to carry the bag instead of wearing it on my back like a sail.

I hadn't seen a soul, until a man with a foreign accent approached me from the side of the building. He was looking for a friend at the marina. "He's been swept out to high seas if he stuck around," I wanted to tell the guy, but I only warned him against walking amidst the storm surge, advising him that the whirlpools from open manhole covers would suck a person into the storm drains. He continued to wade across the water, anyway, and so I clicked away, framing him as he made his way through foamy waves and wind. The wind and rain began to diminish as the remaining feeder bands became fewer and milder. It had cleared to where I could see the individual feeder bands as they approached over the water.

I used a long piece of broken brass railing to probe the ground in front of me as I methodically waded in the calf-deep water toward the marina, shooting now at a machine-gun pace. Bending palm trees swaying in thick sheets of rain, large waves crashing into the docks and white-capped flood waters. These were scenes of which I had only dreamed. The years of planning and mental rehearsals were paying off. I was also bursting with joy over the absence of other journalists. I had expected the standard media frenzy.

Boats that had been tied down sustained heavy damage. Boats were torn apart, smashed into others, sunk or washed ashore by the storm surge. The beautiful yacht I had observed was battered, its bow resting against the concrete shell of the dock. Damage to the docks was so complete that it was difficult to recall where, on Sunday, I had stood for my "before" images. Taking the "after" pictures was a challenge.

As a final rain band hit, I shot a couple of bending palm trees, the marina centered in the background. "The cover of *Life* Magazine," I half-jokingly boasted to a man standing nearby. Before I left the marina, I ran into the two men who had been waiting in the garage to check on their boat. What they discovered was a direct hit. A chunk of a telephone pole had impaled the hull.

After the last squall, I walked south toward the Dinner Key Marina, working my way through debris. Boat parts, clothing, dead fish. I even stepped over a photo album opened to a swollen wet page showing a bearded man making a toast on the deck of his boat. A bottle of Dom Perignon appeared at my feet. Sadly, when I reached for this profound memento, I found it was cracked open on the other side.

Between the two marinas, the bone-chilling screams of a woman froze me in my tracks. I headed toward the screams.

The Dinner Key Marina had suffered no less. Boat owners criss-crossed the fractured docks, peering into the soup of ship parts. I found the woman who was responsible for the screams—standing next to her destroyed boat. One man threw his arms upward and openly thanked God after finding that his yacht had been spared. I overheard someone say another part of south Florida had been "completely destroyed" by the hurricane. I quickly headed back towards the garage.

Mike and Steve had left, obviously concerned about their homes. Mike, it would turn out, returned to a home severely damaged. My last mission at Fort Andrew was a quick self-portrait. I drove through the debris and was relieved to see an unobstructed exit. The screaming madman had vanished.

Shark Tank

Returning to Coral Gables was like putting together one of those 10,000-piece jigsaw puzzles. Fallen trees, power poles and large pieces of construction material blocked roads. I turned the heater on full blast and put my main camera next to the vent, in an effort to dry it out. I listened to the radio and took notes of potential photo opportunities.

I made it back to the Howard Johnson's. It had suffered damage from uprooted trees, and there was neither electricity nor

top: Andrew's debris blocks a road in a Homestead neighborhood

bottom: Damage in the Homestead, Florida area

running water. I used the water in the sink to wash my face and clean my war wounds. A safety pin from my shaving kit closed a gaping hole in my pants. The cool, soft sheets were calling out to me, and my instinct was to dive in and take a quick nap. No way. Any break in my adrenaline-induced work ethic would be the end of the day. I got back in the car and drove south toward the Cutler Ridge and Homestead areas, where the most damage was reported.

The destruction became increasingly vivid as I drove south on U.S. 1 into the Cutler Ridge area. Virtually every building along the highway was damaged. Some were completely leveled. In the surrounding neighborhoods, people walked around like zombies, going nowhere, or I suppose, having nowhere to go. I was taking a telephoto shot of a road covered by power poles when a group of teens approached me and asked for water. I told them I didn't have any, but one tried to open the passenger-side door to my car. I had kept the car in drive and my foot on the accelerator, so the moment the fellow grabbed the door handle, I spun away. In the rearview mirror, my petitioner/assailant picked up an object and hurled it at me.

I pulled into a mall parking lot after noticing looters running from the main entrance. I pointed my camera out the window and at two teens who were stopped across from the car. "Are you a cop?" asked one breathlessly.

"No, I'm a news photographer," I told them.

"Don't take our pictures, man. We're wanted," he responded, and then noted, "Hey, there's still some film in there."

I looked at the bounty in their hands. It appeared more trash than treasure, including a large display bottle of perfume. The bottle was filled with colored water, not perfume, I told him, and it sure wasn't worth being arrested over. He twisted the top off the crystal decanter and smelled the contents. Laughing and cursing at the same time, he hurled the bottle across the parking lot. It skidded along until it hit a curb and shattered. Just then a police car pulled into the lot, and the kids took off, still laughing. I drove on, not wanting to become a suspect

or a victim myself. It was sad, uplifting and always intriguing to watch as Andrew brought out the best and worst of humanity.

Down the road a couple of miles, I stopped again to photograph a National Guardsman with an M-16 rifle standing guard at a damaged bank. Even though I had my press passes prominently displayed, my equipment bag, my blood-speckled clothing and unshaven appearance made me a candidate for a 10 Most Wanted List. I needed to be sure I wasn't taken for a looter myself.

In the same shopping center, there was what appeared to be a record store. I say "appeared" because, whatever it had been, it was no longer. It had been thoroughly looted. Even the shelving was gone. I climbed a pile of wreckage to take my shot when I heard the wail of sirens. A helicopter zoomed overhead, and a National Guard contingent headed across the parking lot towards me. I thought for sure that I was going to be arrested. Seconds later, a long line of new, official-type cars pulled into the parking lot and stopped in front of the store. Behind these vehicles were a line of police motorcycles and unmarked patrol cars. I knew what was coming.

President Bush tours Homestead area damage. August 1992.

As I dug through my gear, a man in a suit approached and gave me the once-over, paying particular attention to my press passes. I explained that I didn't always look this way; he smiled, accepted my presence and headed back. I awaited for whom I was sure would be the governor of Florida on a perfunctory tour of the storm area. Then the car doors opened and out stepped George Bush. I had photographed him before, but this situation was completely different. With the exception of a television crew that was in the parking lot, there were no other journalists in sight. I was excited to think that I was the only photojournalist present. "Wow," I thought. "My ship has come in. I get the prez to myself."

Not to be. This was photo-op time. A bus had emerged from the endless caravan. I called it the "shark tank." This tourist-type bus contained the most aggressive and pompous media on earth. A swarm of journalists emerged from the bus and formed an impregnable circle around the President, offering more protection than the Secret Service. I did, however, hold my ground and got my pictures.

Though I didn't get my moment of glory with George, I did get included on a news feed. My family and friends in Tucson saw me on TV and learned that I was still alive and shooting.

Warren Faidley at the marina as Andrew exits

The remainder of the evening was spent journeying through south Florida, stopping and shooting until the light faded. I did not want to be anywhere near this chaotic scene when darkness fell. I was contemplating the great images I had as I made my way to the hotel. That's when Andrew made one last attempt to keep me from going home.

I took a detour in the dusk and, for a second, was certain I saw something in the road ahead. I locked the brakes and swerved to a stop into the left lane. In my lane, a partially collapsed billboard structure hung some

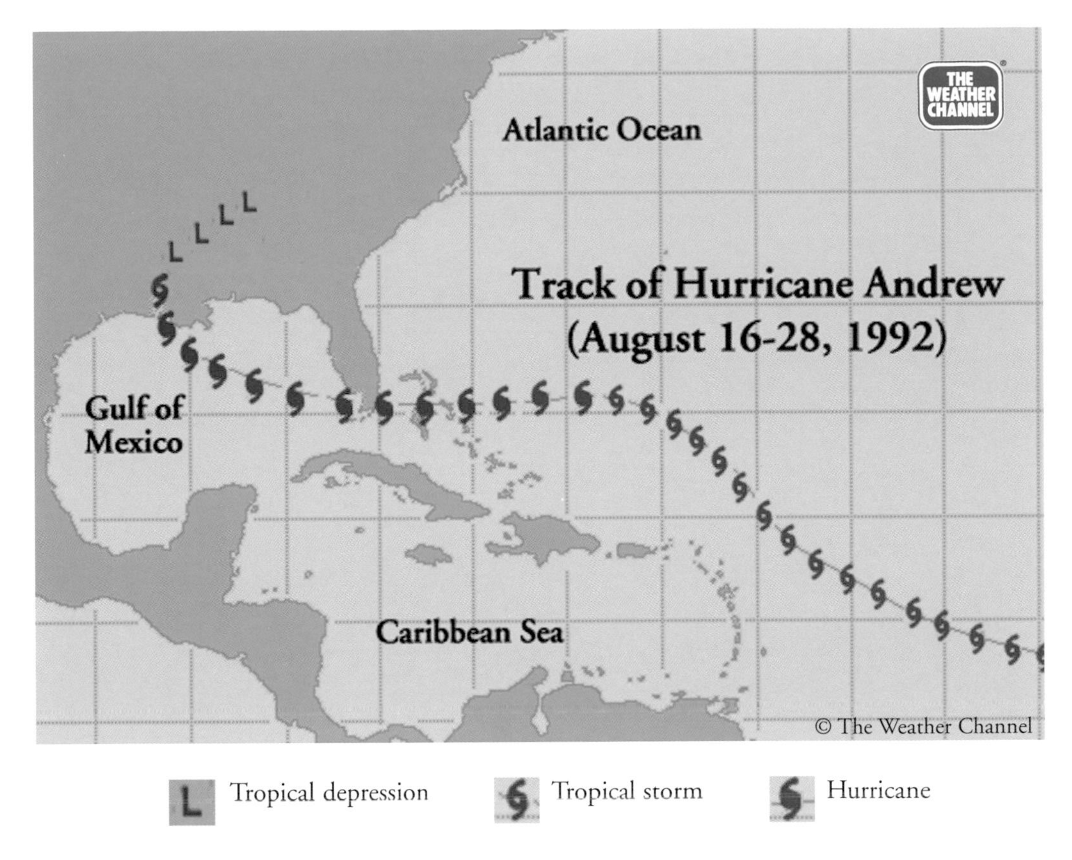

four feet off the roadway. A municipal maintenance truck stopped moments later to close the road. I had won my final skirmish with Andrew.

I spent the next 10 hours in a deep sleep. I would have slept longer had it not been for the buzzing of chain saws cutting away at a distorted landscape.

As for the bending palms I shot in the marina—they made it to the cover of *Life* Magazine.

Wedges and Stovepipes

As we drove through the mountains of New Mexico following our 1992 tornado chase, I told Tom, "I need a vehicle designed just for chasing."

The travel schemes for our earliest tornado chases were simple. I loaded my small sports car, a rental, or Tom's Blues Brothers clone (a police sedan in its previous life) with a half-empty camera bag, three days of clothing, a pile of dog-eared, gas-station road maps, a full gas tank, and we headed east.

We had no communications equipment for relaying information to the National Weather Service, little room for safely stowing delicate camera gear, and no four-wheel drive for slick, muddy roads. Something had to change.

One of seven tornadoes intercepted during the May 5, 1993 outbreak in Texas and Oklahoma

Shadow Chaser

In March of 1993, I took delivery of a midnight black, 4x4, sport utility truck, which I proceeded to partially disassemble in my garage. The list of equipment I added was extensive: a front-mounted video camera system which could tape through the front windshield, several radios and scanners capable of transmitting and receiving chase frequencies, a color monitor for receiving local television reports, special bays for stowing equipment, a long-range cellular phone system that would interface with my laptop for accessing weather data on the fly, a complete digital weather computer center capable of measuring everything from dew points to wind speeds, security and safety equipment, and a host of accessories that would make chasing productive, safe and comfortable.

For a month, I worked night and day preparing the "Shadow Chaser," as I christened it late one evening after Megamouth, my one-toothed cat and overseer of operations, knocked a glass of wine over on the hood. On April 15, my self-imposed deadline, I rolled the Shadow Chaser out of the garage and took it on a shakedown cruise down Interstate 10. The first trucker who saw it called it the "porcupine" because of the six radio/television antennas protruding from the roof.

The overall planning and organizing of a two-month chase that would cover hundreds of thousands of square miles required meticulous attention. I obsess about lists. Equipment and supplies had to be bought or designed and built. Checklists had to be updated, computer forecasting and communications equipment was upgraded and tested. Financial and travel arrangements were made. Press releases were sent and news interviews scheduled.

left: The Shadow Chaser™ and Warren Faidley

right: Warren Faidley reviews a check list in the Shadow Chaser™.

One of the critical and tedious pre-chase duties was checking and updating maps and radio frequencies for at least seven states. Roads and weather information are the lifeblood of a chase. Maps are often vital to success. When I look back over the years, the availability, or lack, of a road leading to a storm is often the difference in making—or breaking—a chase. An inaccurate list of roads, or the failure to receive weather data such as warnings, is playing with one's life. When chasers gather, there are always the inevitable stories about the storm that got away or the one that nearly killed someone because a road simply ended or was misprinted on a map.

There is another peril that has nothing to do with maps or road networks. Forget tornadoes and lightning—the greatest hazards are the drives of 300 to 600 miles a day. Dust clouds, drunks, dark cows, hydroplaning, narrow roads and slow-moving farm machinery are riskier than Mother Nature. Small white crosses and skid marks leading to oily piles of shattered glass serve as constant reminders of those dangers.

It was late April, the Shadow Chaser was ready, and I was aching to get back on the road.

OUTBREAK!

CHASE LOG: MAY 5, 1993. AMARILLO, TEXAS.

8:05 a.m. The slam of a car door startles me from my sleep. I'm instantly alert, as I have not forgotten that last night's forecast showed the potential for a promising chase day. I waste no time jumping from bed to take my first glance between the cracks of the smelly motel drapes.

Only a couple of cars remain in the lot. People don't seem to hang around here for long. There is an encouraging, brisk, south wind bending the dry grass over in the surrounding fields. Small cumulus clouds, the early predecessors to storm clouds, reflect off the shiny black hood of the Shadow Chaser.

8:55 a.m. I connect my laptop computer to the telephone jack and dial into a forecasting company to get my first weather fix. The computer screen flickers and fills with forecast and meteorological data from throughout the region. I scan the texts and numbers, with the knowledge that it's too early to make a definite chase forecast. Nonetheless, the data is exciting. There is a substantial probability of severe weather within a one-hundred-mile radius of Amarillo. "It looks juicy today," I yell to Tom.

Meanwhile, Tom, satisfied that his cameras are ready for action, has turned to the customary morning ritual of reorganizing our main equipment. Every day, each piece of equipment, plus the supplies, must be checked, cleaned and returned to the exact, strategic place. During the heat of a chase, there is no time to fumble around looking for a missing lens or roll of film. Luck is, as someone once said, "the residue of design."

10:15 a.m. We begin the task of preparing and loading the Shadow Chaser. Tom re-attaches the six antennas, remote camera mount and the wind anemometer support and cups. I make a quick sweep through the front of the truck, removing Moon Pie wrappers and empty water bottles before I install the radios and electronic equipment. After a quick radio test, I check under the hood, glance at the tires, check the wipers, headlights and emergency equipment.

The "money lady" passes through the lot and stops across from us. A rough-looking woman in her late forties, she's a con artist who uses the same line and sad facial expressions every time, verbatim. "Excuse me, sir, my purse was stolen, and I've got to get to Dallas to take care of my children. Would you be so kind as to lend me $20 for gas?" Her memory must be shot, for she never remembers us, even though I feed her the same line. "A twister took off with my wallet." Suddenly, she recognizes us, her face turns sour, and she speeds away.

10:30 a.m. The morning checklist is nearly complete. A man walks by, notices the "Severe Storm Interceptors/Spotter" emblem on the truck door, and peppers us with the usual questions: "Are we going to have any storms today? Why do you chase storms? What's the best storm you've ever witnessed?"

10:45 a.m. Tom carries out the critical duty of cleaning the insects off the windshield. I notice that the cumulus clouds have thinned. My spirits dim a little as we head down the road to fill the gas tank.

The CB radio is quiet now. Last night it hummed with cheap entertainment. One guy was trying to sell "wake up" drugs to truckers. On another channel, a "lot lizard" (trucker lingo for a prostitute) was soliciting. But the most captivating broadcaster was a man who possesses the foulest mouth in the world. He is the undisputed king of profanity. Most of the time, he's silent, monitoring the airwaves, but the moment he hears a trucker say something that displeases him, the mouth goes off like an A-bomb.

His radio is so powerful that it drowns out everyone for miles, leaving him to dominate the airwaves as he spits and swears for a few minutes until he goes silent, resting up for the next round. I once asked him to "talk slower" so I could tape his dialog for a friend back home. He scorched the airwaves.

12:20 p.m. We arrive at the NWS office in Amarillo. Inside, we are greeted by José Garcia, the Meteorologist In Charge. José is a wonderful supervisor who has made the Amarillo office one of the best in the Alley. The Amarillo office also has one of the best spotter networks in the region, with hundreds of trained volunteer "skywarn" spotters who relay storm information to the office via ham radios and mobile phones. I sit down in the office library and mark my forecast sheet with green, purple, red and blue pencils, denoting winds, moisture, pressures and temperatures. As I draw, the page becomes a colored, confusing maze of squiggly lines and numbers. It is not art, however. It is a clear message; the page is trying to tell me something.

There is a relatively high risk of severe weather in the original 100-mile range of Amarillo. This forecast is supported by the presence of a strong jet stream overhead, an ample supply of surface moisture, and a weather disturbance moving into the area.

While I continue to study my own information, similar data is being carefully scrutinized by the Severe Local Storms Unit, or SELS*, at the National Severe Storms Forecast Center (NSSFC), in Kansas City. The NSSFC is the central nerve center for severe weather forecasting in the United States. At least twice a day during the storm season, SELS issues detailed outlooks for the affected areas.

The probability of severe weather is broken down into four "risk" ratings: approaching severe, slight chance of severe, moderate risk and high risk. The morning SELS discussion produces a ranking of moderate risk in our forecast area. It adds, "Isolated supercells are expected to become tornadic."

In spite of the early, foreboding indications of severe storms, the event is not expected until later in the afternoon when the maximum surface heating assists in convection. As the day wears on, and weather information is updated, my suspect forecast area will shrink into a manageable target area. Having time on our side, we decide to return to the city and have the oil changed on the Shadow Chaser.

2:30 p.m. We return to the weather office to examine the latest data and to make our final chase decision. The best area appears to be north of Amarillo, extending into portions of southwestern Kansas. The likelihood of severe weather becomes greater with each hour's data. Dew points and southerly surface winds are increasing, barometric pressures are falling. Tom and I consult each other on distances and highway options. We aren't worried about fatigue; we drive 300 to 400 miles a day during "high" season, and we have barely moved today.

3:30 p.m. While we're waiting for the 4 p.m. data, José gives us a long-awaited tour of the newly installed Doppler radar, officially known as the WSR-88-D or Weather Surveillance Radar, 1988-Doppler. This high-tech color radar can record cumulative rainfall amounts, measure winds aloft and dissect a thunderstorm's innards. But the main feature of this radar, to a chaser, is its ability to detect wind motion within a storm, the telltale signs of tornadic rotation. If such rotation is

---

** SELS was reorganized into the Storm Prediction Center in 1996.*

detected, the system can sound an automatic alarm, based on predetermined algorithms programmed into the main computer. Fortunately for us, we do not need a multi-million-dollar Doppler unit in the Shadow Chaser— the data is available through private computer links via my cellular phone and computer.

Yet another fantastic feature of the sensitive radar is its ability to detect low-level weather features such as the often unstable boundaries between opposing air masses. One of these boundaries is the dryline. Within the next few hours, the new radar will receive a monumental christening.

3:40 p.m. As we admire the Doppler, a forecaster sounds a warning. On a large color monitor, he observes a strange radar signature—a long, snaky green line—running over a hundred miles from the southeast toward the northwest. We gather around the radar monitor and observe this incredible sight. A significant dryline merges—almost directly on top of us.

4:15 p.m. Satellite images and the Doppler show small clouds developing in the northwestern portion of the Texas panhandle, where the green lines on the radar screen had started to merge. Our chase must start immediately. We thank José on the way out, tell him we are headed north and will be on the skywarn frequency.

We head east on Highway 60. I call KFDA-TV in Amarillo to talk with fellow chaser "Doppler" Dave Oliver. Dave Oliver is one of the few television weather-persons in the world who has given several live weather reports with actual tornadoes in the background. We often consult with each other when a particular piece of hell is about to break loose. "It looks good where you're going," Dave advises. "I'd be there myself except that I have to do the weather at five. You'll probably run into our chase team. They're already on their way."

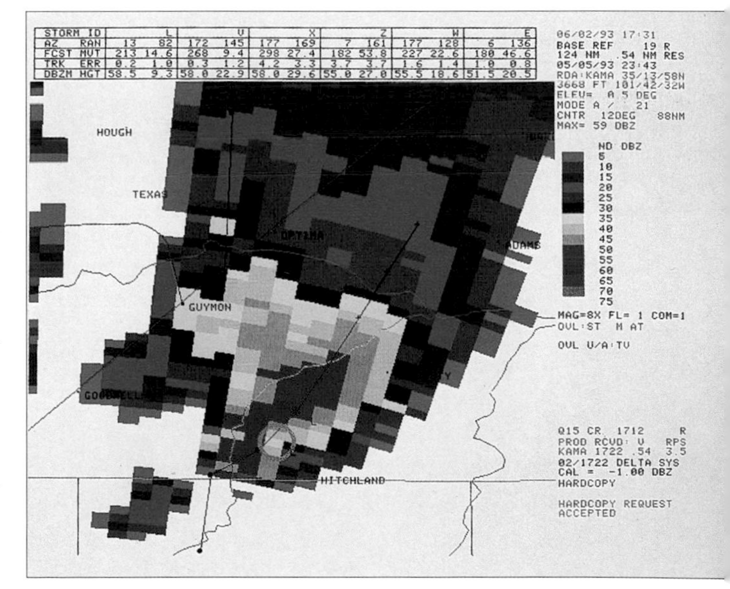

Doppler radar printout from the May 5, 1993 tornado outbreak. Gold circle indicates a mesocyclone (our tornado).

4:20 p.m. I am studying the Texas map book when the weather-alert alarm sounds. Tornado Watch # 201 is issued, which includes our target area of the Texas and Oklahoma panhandles. Some animals detect weather change through their tails. I get this familiar feeling in my stomach. Something is about to happen.

4:38 p.m. We pass through Panhandle and turn north on Highway 207. Though the sky is hazy from high humidity, we see storm anvil tops, fanning out to the northeast for miles. The storms have begun to explode somewhere in Sherman County, Texas, 50 miles to the north, we suspect. Instead of driving into an area where clouds may obstruct our view, we opt for more secure guidance, a live television radar report from Dave during the 5 p.m. news. We stop on a small hill north of the town of Panhandle to get our report.

5:15 p.m. Dave explains that storms are rapidly building near Gruver, Texas. Radar shows a line of greens and yellows, and in the center is a large red blob (a good storm signature) about 50 miles north. "Nothing severe yet," he states, "but we're going to have to watch this real close."

The often beautiful, enchanting Plains

"Let's go," I tell Tom. We jump into the truck, and we're storm-bound.

Neither of us speaks. Tom stares at the road, and my mind drifts away from the chase. I peer at the tranquil, endless landscape of flowing fields broken only by an occasional farm house or the distant white tower of a grain elevator. What a backdrop for such evil storms! Off to the right, a farmer plows his field. We pass a dilapidated farmhouse with a swing on the front porch, and I recall my sickbed dream in Amarillo three years ago. I remember what storm chaser Joel Ewing always says when he sees such a time-weathered building in the Alley, "If only that building could talk, think of the storms it would tell us about!".

5:36 p.m. A radio station in Guymon, Oklahoma reports that a severe thunderstorm warning has been issued, and the storm is now less than 30 miles away. We are out of range of the NWS radio in Amarillo, so we must rely on AM and FM radio reports, plus skywarn storm spotters on the ham radio.

6:05 p.m. Approaching Gruver, the overcast skies and haze break apart to reveal the back side of a massive, and developed, storm just a few miles away. Suddenly, the scanner locks onto a loud, clear transmission from KFDA's mobile chase unit. "We have a very, very large funnel cloud coming from this storm, just outside of Gruver." I look down at the map and tell Tom, "That's about eight miles away. Punch it, let's go!"

6:10 p.m. Just outside of town, we see the bright red KFDA van to the side of the road, as a cameraman aims to the northwest. A large gray-white funnel cloud hangs from the dark cloud base. I grab the two-meter radio microphone and call in a report to the NWS in Amarillo. Meanwhile, Tom has pulled the truck off the road. The funnel soon retreats into the storm. "Did it touch down?" Tom asks. "Don't know," they respond.

6:19 p.m. We drive north, parallel to the backside of the storm. The entire agitated base reorganizes, darkens and rotates. Overhead, the solid white clouds tower into a sprawling canopy, resembling the top of a mushroom. Excitement overwhelms me, but my gut is in a knot. Anyone in the path of this storm is in grave danger. I check the automatic settings and film counter on my cameras.

6:28 p.m. We follow the storm for as long as we can. It slowly moves toward us and starts to cross the highway. The KFDA van pulls up behind us, and we stop to let the storm cross the road. Tom's motor drive whirls away. "There's going to be a big tornado in a few minutes," I yell to Tom and the other chasers. The furious clouds boil overhead.

A semi behind us comes to an abrupt halt, and the driver opens the window and shouts, "Hey! Can I drive under that thing?"

"Wouldn't if I were you," I tell him. He waits on the road as the swirling mass crosses the highway.

Seconds later, just as the driver climbs in his cab, a large rental car goes screaming by, sliding for a moment on the soft shoulder and almost losing control.

Approaching the base of a dark storm

"Idiot!" Tom yells out. The truck driver leans out the window and yells a mouthful of expletives. The car, full of well-known outlaw chasers, continues north. An arm emerges from the window, the horn blares and we're flashed a thumbs-up signal.

"If I catch that son of a bitch, I'd kill him!" the truck driver shouts in his drawl. The car passes right under the swirling clouds. The outlaws fade from sight to parts unknown as a small finger-like funnel cloud pokes out from the clouds and vanishes.

I reach into the truck and grab the microphone, "KB5-JJB, this is KB7-TVO," I transmit. "Go ahead," responds the Amarillo spotter coordinator. "This is Warren. I've got a large area of organized rotation, about eight miles north of Gruver, just west of Highway 207."

"Roger that, Warren. The radar confirms your report. I'll pass the information on to José. Thanks," they respond.

6:35 p.m. I dread missing my photo opportunities, and this is a fear today. Not that the storm is moving too fast; rather, roads in this area are not extensive. Most run due east or north, and storms don't adhere to the U.S. Interstate system. Storm chasing often becomes a Herculean game of chess.

I plot a course that allows us to keep up with a storm. Tom loads up his equipment and turns the truck around. We begin zig-zagging through a maze of unmarked farm roads just a few miles south of the Oklahoma panhandle. With our storm safely to the west, moving in a north-northeast direction, I reason that we can stay close to the updraft without putting ourselves in the direct path of a tornado.

6:40 p.m. Suddenly, from the center of the swirling clouds, less than a mile away, a large cone-shaped funnel forms. Within a few minutes the cone lengthens and becomes a long, dull white funnel, shaped like an elephant's trunk. It quickly touches the ground, officially becoming a tornado. As the main tornado drops, a series of wispy vortices begin to dance around the main shaft, forming a dome of dust and debris over the green fields. I transmit again, "KB5-JJB, this is KB7-TVO. We've got a large, multi-vortex tornado on the ground, about three or four miles near the state line."

6:45 p.m. Other storm spotters report the tornado. "It's now on the ground and appears to be getting larger and larger," one spotter reports. We travel Highway 207, the tornado to our left. I videotape over Tom's shoulder, and he occasionally raises his camera to the window and squeezes off a few frames.

"Now that's a tornado!" Tom says. The tornado is going through a metamorphosis, from an orgy of intertwined white vortices into a long funnel, shaped like a stovepipe. Soon it debuts in its most menacing appearance, a gray, wedge-shaped vortex, widening to a half-mile in diameter. I glance down at the maps in order to plot an intercept course. To my dismay, both Guymon and Hooker, Oklahoma are within the possible path.

6:51 p.m. Rounding a corner on 207, somewhere just inside the Oklahoma panhandle, the road turns slightly to the northwest. The tornado begins to cross the road about a mile in front of us. "Look at that," Tom says, referring to the photographic qualities, "a beautiful white twister over a bright green field. Want to stop?"

The tornado takes on a "cone" shape. Oklahoma, May 5, 1993.

"NO! NO!" I shout. "Keep going, punch it. Let's get close to this baby and get some good shots!"

"I'd say here—or we're going to miss it," Tom insists.

"NO," I tell him. "Keep going. Peak this small hill. We're not going to miss it." The engine races as Tom reluctantly floors the pedal, and we close in on the vortex. We slide to a stop on the dirt shoulder of the highway. The tornado is less than a half-mile down the road. We jump out of the truck, swing open the back doors, grab our gear, and start to shoot. Years of preparation and tens of thousands of miles come down to a moment like this—the most picturesque tornado we have ever seen.

The video camera I keep mounted on a tripod needed only to be set on the ground, aligned (at the viewfinder) and turned on. I reach for my still camera and fire away, going through a 36-exposure roll of film in less than fifteen seconds. The problem with our tornado is the lack of light, due in part to another tornadic supercell forming about thirty miles to our west. A thick humid haze makes the vortex appear diffused through our lenses, and a stiff wind rocks the tripods. "I don't believe it," I shout over to Tom. "We've got the best tornado in the world, and we can't get a good shot.'

"We need contrast," Tom says.

"Then we'll have to go further down the road and get closer to it," I yell. We pack up and travel northeast along a bumpy dirt road with our tornado churning up the plains next to us.

6:53 p.m. We turn off the paved highway and chase the storm from the dirt roads once again. This allows us to stay next to the tornado, although we keep an eye out for an occasional boulder or enormous pothole. One error at the wheel and these chasers are going to watch their careers pass in front of them from a roadside ditch.

Each time we approach an intersection, we both scan the roads and shout "clear." Soon we are less than a mile from the fat, white tornado. All at once, we're hit by strong, inflow jet winds feeding into the tornadic circulation. Tom fights the steering wheel for a second, and we're nearly forced off the road. The computer screen that records the outside wind gusts shows 129 mph. Compensating for our relatively slow traveling speed at the time, the wind gust had to be over 90 mph!

6:55 p.m. Tom looks to our left and suddenly yells, "Look! We've got a second tornado forming right here!"

I look over. Sure enough, a debris cloud is forming on the ground below the flanking line of clouds feeding into the main storm. "It's ripping up a fence," Tom says, as the small vortex, without a distinguishable funnel cloud above, tears across the dry fields only a few hundred yards from us. It yanks up a section of barbed wire fence as if it were uprooting a shallow weed after a heavy rain. It hurls the fence skyward.

"Slow down, Tom," I say. "We don't want to get hit by that devil." Moments later the debris cloud diminishes.

7:05 p.m. We make our way through the confusing network of unmarked, dirt farm roads, and we finally come to a dead end. The tornado is still twirling away in front of us. We pull up next to a mud-caked pickup truck. Inside are two grungy-looking men wearing sweat-stained, straw cowboy hats. "Do you know if there are any roads going north from here?" I ask.

"Yep, we sure do," one of them says, gulping down a swig of beer. "How much you willing to pay us?" the other one says, half-laughing and exposing a mouthful of yellow teeth. I think they are joking, at first, but the other one adds: "You heard him, if you want out of here, you gonna pay."

"Thanks anyway," I respond politely, hoping to avoid any confrontation. "Jerks," I murmur under my breath.

7:14 p.m. We backtrack, and the tornado disappears into the back of the storm, behind a sheet of rain. Reports of our tornado, and others nearby, are broadcast over the radio and scanner.

7:21 p.m. No sooner do we turn east on Highway 3, than we are greeted by a long snaky tornado crossing a few miles in front of us. "Hey, it's the Wizard of Oz tornado," Tom says, "and it's the shot we want."

Once again we're driving directly toward a tornado. A mile away, we stop, because it appears to be weakening. We shoot it before it completely disappears. The moment Tom stops, I fly out the door and place the bottom of my still camera

against the hood to keep it steady. I go through another roll of film, varying the exposures as much as I can in the poor light. Seconds later the funnel retreats back into the dark clouds. We continue east and just to the side of where the tornado crossed. The clouds spin violently, preparing for another round.

7:50 p.m. The town of Hooker, Oklahoma has been spared. The tornadic storms, in their constant transformations, pass directly between Guymon and Hooker. We slide to a stop at the corner gas station with brakes screeching and lights flashing. The people gathered around the store gawk at us—I'm reminded of the crowd scene from *Ghostbusters.* I quickly fill the tank, then we scream off west toward the storm's re-forming updraft.

8:05 p.m. Tom slows down at an intersection. I look to the northeast and see a long stovepipe-shaped tornado coming from the back of a second storm cell. It has formed to the west of the original storm. "I don't believe it," I say. "Two large supercells, both dropping tornadoes everywhere!" We turn north at the intersection on an unmarked, paved road, and once again we're heading towards a twister. Is this our fourth of the day? Our fifth? I've lost track.

Tom's "Wizard of Oz" *tornado. Oklahoma, May 5, 1993.*

8:08 p.m. The stovepipe tornado disappears into the clouds before we can shoot it. The sinking sun and the dark storm clouds, which absorbed any extra light, have now made it too dark to shoot. I'm also concerned that the fading light could conceal any new tornadoes. A tornado may intercept *us* if we're not careful.

8:12 p.m. We continue our slow trek, close to the Kansas border. The pavement has become a total mess from a construction project. Our equipment bounces and rattles around the truck. I look around to ensure that none of our cameras or lenses are in danger of being crushed. Five miles down the center of the road, in the dusk, we notice a suspicious cloud looming over the road. "Whoa. Stop. STOP!" I yell to Tom. All at once a grayish, wispy funnel cloud forms in what must have been the same location of the earlier stovepipe. "We've got a funnel forming right in front of us," I dictate in the video camera's microphone. The KFDA crew pulls in front of us and begins shooting the rough-appearing vortex. Within seconds, the funnel stops rotating and the clouds dissipate.

8:18 p.m. In the twilight, we witness two more tornadoes to the distant east, including another wedge that we watch as it churns into Kansas. We head back to Amarillo, listening to live radio reports about the storms. "With as many tornadoes as we have had on the ground tonight, it's a miracle that none of them have hit a populated area," says one reporter. I use the mobile phone to call in our motel reservations to Amarillo.

12:35 a.m. I try to sleep, but the day continues to play through my mind like a movie. Things happened so fast that, from the seven 36-exposure rolls that I shot, I remember only a few. I'm concerned about the exposures, because I shot by instinct and don't remember any exposure settings. I'm sure I checked them subconsciously—or did I? These worries taunt me until I fall asleep, and they resume when I wake up. I will purge them only when my film is processed.

May 9th began with the promise of another severe weather day. I never would have suspected what was waiting in the midst of the next chase.

Weather data indicated that the Wichita Falls area would be the best place to chase. But my intuition told me to go north. Tom drove as I scoured the data and plotted a course towards Gruver. We arrived in Gruver 90 minutes later. A small storm did develop but soon fizzled. The day was beginning to look like a bust, so we decided to make our way back to Amarillo.

About a mile down Farm Road 278, I spotted what appeared to be a plastic supermarket bag in the middle of the road. Tom maneuvered to avoid it. I suddenly yelled out to him, as he was already braking hard, "What the … hey … LOOK OUT… HIT THE BRAKES!" The truck came to a sliding stop, and I leaped out. In the center of the highway was a small boy. I ran toward him.

He wiggled and waved his arms, as if he didn't have a care in the world. I ran to the nearest house while Tom moved the boy off the road, just as a pickup truck raced by from the opposite direction. Tom asked the toddler where his father was, and the boy pointed off toward a nearby field.

I pounded on the door of the first house I came to. A man answered. "Do you have a little boy dressed in overalls?" "Yes," the man replied, his face stricken with panic. "He's fine," I said. "We found him in the middle of the road." "Oh, my good Jesus!" the man exclaimed as he bolted out the door and darted toward the highway.

The toddler had wandered out of the house and onto the road. The father, in a virtual state of shock, thanked us profusely.

The Sky Is Falling

Chase Log: June 2, 1993.
Amarillo, Texas.

I'm still around, someone once told me, because I have at least one diligent guardian angel who watches over me. No argument here.

I'm also alive because I know when to quit. I survived long enough during the early chase days to learn that every storm has a boundary that separates the world of safety from a chaotic and unpredictable domain of mortal danger, where perception of time and space are dangerously distorted.

I know when to quit, but even so, it's still difficult to let go, especially if the prize is within grasp. While I was shooting a picturesque tornado forming near Pampa, Texas, for example, I stood at my tripod for as long as

Hailstones cover a bare field west of Lubbock, Texas.

I could until the size of hail stones grew so big as to produce painful welts. I departed with a great image but likely missed the best part of the show.

Safe behavior was not on my mind this morning at 8, when I got out of bed, slipped on sandals and took my habitual glance out the window. The flag in front of the motel was blowing straight out from a strong southeastern wind. This was a good sign. Stiff winds were importing moisture from the Gulf of Mexico and providing low-level wind shear, which is good for tornadogenesis. Overhead, a stream of feathery cirrus clouds denoted upper-level winds and the possibility of a disturbance. Where would all of these ingredients come together to create the right storm?

Tom and I decided to forego breakfast after completing a later-than-usual ritual packing and checking of equipment. We were headed to the Amarillo NWS office, where we planned to meet John Monteverdi, our friend and fellow chaser.

We were met at the office by Ed Andrade, one of the best severe-weather forecasters in the Alley. I could tell by the half-serious smile on his face that something was up. "You guys are going to love this," he said as he handed us a computer printout. The National Severe Storms Forecast Center's (NSSFC) storm outlook included a "high-risk" of severe thunderstorms over the eastern portions of Colorado and western Kansas. This area was well within striking range and was networked with decent roads.

When one of these days comes along in the hot zone, I try to suppress my enthusiasm and remain cautiously optimistic. High-risk days have a way of going bust; I've spent more than one of them on a deserted road, in the middle of nowhere, watching an extremely ordinary day. Nonetheless, the NSSFC would not issue such a forecast unless there was a good probability of serious weather.

Meteorologist Ed Andrade (left) and Warren Faidley, at the National Weather Service office in Amarillo, Texas

I read the outlook text, which included the PDS —particularly dangerous situation—coding. "You ready to go back to Oklahoma for another outbreak?" I asked Tom. It had been just over a month and 9,000 miles since our May 5 tornadic free-for-all in Oklahoma.

As I busied myself marking up the latest data with my colored pencils, we were joined by chaser brethren. The additions to our morning brain pool included veteran chaser John Monteverdi, a Professor of Meteorology from San Francisco State University and his chase partner Thom Trimble, an engineer from northern California. John and Thom spend their spring vacations roaming the Plains in search of tornadoes for both personal and scientific reasons.

Once, while we were engaged in a three-vehicle chase near Plainview, Texas, John used his expertise at map reading to save our hides. He diverted us from an approaching vortex by directing us straight towards a roaring hail shaft. I worried that John was taking us from the frying pan and tossing us into the fire, but it was the only way out. "We have one chance, Warren," he had told me over the radio. "Go two miles straight towards the hail, and there'll be a road that turns east, away from the hail and the tornado." I'd had many a close call with hail before, and I knew darn well that it could turn a car into a battered heap. Just before we impacted the lime-green hailshafts, we came to the intersection and escaped.

While I was discussing my morning weather maps with John, the office library was graced by the presence of Marty Feely. Marty is unique. He is one of the most colorful chasers to roam the Plains. Sporting his trademark rust-colored beard, shorts and drug store sunglasses, he takes any odd job he can find to maintain his spring chasing habit. In 1993, Marty devised a clever way to chase and make money simultaneously. "Whirlwind Tours" takes vacationers on tornado-hunting expeditions through the Alley. His contract stipulates that there are no guarantees.

Professor John Monteverdi (left) and Warren Faidley plan a chase.

For years Marty has been a member of a relatively unknown, elite group of 30 to 40 seasoned "hobbyist chasers" who return to the Alley each spring.

Hobbyist chasers pursue storms for many reasons. Some are college students who study meteorology; others are weather buffs driven by scientific curiosity and a lust for travel. Unlike the dreaded outlaw chasers, the majority of serious hobbyists also serve as weather spotters, calling in reports by ham radio or cellular phone. Almost all are amateur photographers or videographers. A handful of chasers, like John Monteverdi, are both hobbyist and scientist.

These chasers plan their vacation time around the spring season. They show up in the Alley for a week in May, then return home until next year. During the off season, they trade video tapes of their adventures. Chasing has even become a family affair. Phil and Kathy Henry applied their road racing skills and electronics knowledge to form a rare husband-and-wife chase team. Their passion to chase tornadoes resulted in the transformation of Kathy's sport utility truck into a turbo-charged, *Mad Max*-like chase wagon.

Our group gathered in the weather office library-turned-briefing-room and brought each other up-to-date on war stories and gossip. Our brotherhood is small, and we don't see one another often. The best stories are the "close calls" and "the one that got away" or "the biggest storm I've ever seen." And there is always at least one story about the antics of outlaws.

Our conversations soon turned to the day's forecast. While we gathered around the large, oval table, pontificating about what "would, could and should" be, the thought occurred to me: How strange this scene—grown men discussing their plans to battle a storm—would appear to anyone in the real world. Ed Andrade, our NWS liaison, stood by the doorway shaking his head. "You guys better stop sorcering up storms or they'll all just die before you get to them."

"OK, Ed," I said. "Why don't you go chasing with us after your shift is over?"

Storm chaser Phil Henry fine-tunes his satellite dish, used to receive weather data.

"No way," he responded, laughing. "The last time I went chasing with one of you, I nearly got pounded with baseballs [hail]."

We made our final decision by 1 p.m. The first storms would develop in eastern Colorado and move east into Kansas, we believed. Marty and John's crews departed, while Tom and I lagged behind to take a final look at data. Chasers usually agree on general areas but are also governed by their own forecast idiosyncrasies and experience. We would all likely meet again that day in what is called a chaser's convergence, near the biggest, most obvious storm.

Tom and I left after we saw a new satellite loop showing small but suspicious cloud buildups in Baca County, Colorado, 120 miles northwest of Amarillo. These fields of bubbling cumulus clouds often signal the maturing of an explosive atmosphere.

We noticed the first storm clouds at about 4 p.m., some 20 miles from the Oklahoma border on Highway 287. The expanding clouds broke the monotony of a long drive, providing a picturesque view set against the gently flowing green fields and comfortable homesteads.

"Six two of nineteen ninety-three. Four-o-nine p.m. on Highway 287, northbound, about five miles south of the Oklahoma border," I narrated. "First storm clouds of the day have just gone up. We just heard on the radio that a tornado watch has been issued for eastern Colorado."

The mass of clouds developed into a small storm directly in front of us, much to our satisfaction. In less than 30 minutes, the top of the cloud flattened into a small anvil shape. Five miles from the main updraft area, we decided to pull over and watch.

The thunderstorm began to die within 20 minutes. Once solid clouds turned lifeless gray and were quickly devoured by the wind, leaving an orphan anvil floating in the sky like a jelly fish. Diminishing clouds would signal improving weather to the inexperienced. But, to a seasoned chaser, a storm that explodes so rapidly is often a precursor to severe weather.

We continued north and soon saw the solid mass of another storm-in-the-making, 40 miles to the northwest. We knew, in an hour, that this was the real thing. It was well-developed and strengthening rapidly. The top of the storm was

Storm cloud development, from towering cumulus stage to mature stage

covered by a spectacular circular anvil cloud, easily in excess of 50,000 feet. This storm was becoming a supercell, a tempest of such awesome power that it had begun to dominate the atmosphere. Any small cloud mass that tried to challenge the giant was slowly drawn into the storm cells and consumed for fuel.

Supercells frighten and intimidate on looks alone. Their offspring are no less feared. They are known for dropping tornadoes and hailstones that grow to softball-size, falling at 100 mph. Farmers are especially wary of these storms, which produce swaths of hail from 10 to 100 miles long and 10 miles wide and reduce crops to mush. Supercells may move at a snail's pace or at better than 50 mph. The art of intercepting such storms is based largely on intuition and experience, the availability of roads and the love of life.

Supercells are erratic and occasionally become so massive that they defy upper-level steering winds. Instead of moving from a general southwest-to-northeast direction, they can abruptly change course and move toward the east or south. Storms that make this turn are called right-movers and are often associated with extremely dangerous weather. In addition to the unpredictable movement of supercells, massive rain and hail curtains often wrap around the storm's base, concealing a chaser's view of important low-level features, e.g., tornadoes. This often forces a chaser into the nerve-racking and hazardous task of trying to keep slightly ahead of a storm.

Within an hour, we were in striking range of the new storm. There was a feeling of raw energy all around. The storm had become a living, breathing machine. Only a handful of storms reach this stature, developing their own nasty personalities.

We approached cautiously from the rear, rain-free base of the storm from Highway 287, just north of Springfield, Colorado. Tom pulled the Shadow Chaser to the side, alongside John Monteverdi and his partner Thom. "Looks like we have some chaser convergence today," I shouted across to John.

"Where were you guys?" John asked. "We had at least one funnel cloud over here while we approached."

I looked to the northwest and the dark base. The bottom of the cloud was ringed by low-hanging, slowly rotating scud clouds. Tom had already started to fire

away with his still cameras. I used the truck as a wind block for my video camera and tripod. Shortly thereafter, Marty and his client pulled up.

A deputy sheriff arrived and began his own watch, as the center of the storm began to organize. We became concerned that another tornado drop was imminent, in that the storm had already produced several funnels and a possible brief tornado. John, who carried the weight as the professor, convinced the deputy that a tornado warning should be issued. The deputy radioed headquarters.

The storm expanded to the southeast, our direction, and picked up speed. Soon it was crossing Highway 287. Tom and I led the way as our caravan headed east on Highway 160, flanking the storm to the south. This placed us in front of the storm and gave us a magnificent view of the gust front, a dark wedge-shaped cloud that precedes the storm. It is formed as ice-cold air falls from great heights and condenses as it fans out along warm ground. The underside of this cloud feature was a particularly foreboding black and green. The leading edge, which arched across green fields for miles, was lined with small, fang-shaped cloud appendages. I pointed the video camera out the window and filled the viewfinder with this incredible sight. Marty and John disappeared behind us.

A few miles into Kansas, I noticed that the storm was turning, or expanding, to the southeast, deviating from its original course. "Looks like we've got a right mover," I said into the microphone. I pressed the search button on the AM radio, and the search stopped on a high-pitched Emergency Broadcast System (EBS) tone. "I'll bet it's a tornado warning," I told Tom. "The National Weather Service in Dodge City, Kansas, has issued a tornado warning effective until 7:45 p.m. for

top: Chaser convergence in Tornado Alley

right: A gust front approaches.

Morton county in southwest Kansas," the announcer said. "At 7:28, the National Weather Service radar in Dodge City detected a tornado 15 miles southwest of Johnson, moving southeast at 25 mph. This is a dangerous storm. Take action now. Remember that seconds save lives."

I grabbed the road map, aware that the tornado was but a few miles to the southwest, moving in our direction. We needed to intercept and, possibly, avoid the tornado. The main body of the storm appeared to be moving east at 15 to 20 mph. We should continue east, towards Johnson, and then turn south on State Highway 27. This plan, in theory, would allow us to get well in front of the storm before we turned south, putting us in a position to intercept any tornado from a safer location. We would be at the back side of the storm with the tornado moving away from us.

We approached Johnson, observing a gust front and a part of the core of the storm that had crossed the highway behind us. A wall of dark, heavy rain obliterated the view. Unmistakable bright white streaks of hail shafts closed in from behind like curtains. Our fears were heightened when the scanner picked up the static-laden transmission of a deputy somewhere behind us. His car was being bombarded by giant hail, he told the dispatcher urgently.

Tom kept checking the rearview mirror. "I hope Monteverdi and Marty turned around," he said.

I grabbed the video camera again and leaned out the window. I aimed at the opaque hail shafts against the boiling storm, which had turned a foul yellow-green. "You're not going to believe this shot," I told Tom. Tom was more interested in preserving his life than in responding to my enthusiasm. Moments later, I, too, realized that something was wrong.

"You won't want to hear this," I said. "This storm is either collapsing or expanding faster than we're moving." I put the video camera aside and studied the maps. Tom accelerated, but it was for naught. Two miles outside of Johnson, a wall of gusty, blinding dust overtook us.

Through the blowing dust in Johnson, we scanned the sides of the road until we saw the sign marked "State Highway 27 South" and another sign telling us it was 23 miles to Richfield. I sighed in relief, confident I had outwitted yet another storm. We headed south, but after a few miles I cursed myself and felt a knot in my stomach and a lump in my throat. We hadn't outwitted anything. My calculations had failed. We realized we were in serious trouble, with a storm cloud and dust-shrouded tornado bearing down upon us somewhere nearby.

We had periodically discussed the "final option"—abandoning the truck and finding shelter in a ditch—if we couldn't escape a tornado. I reached behind the seat and grabbed my punch-out bag, filled with a week's worth of exposed film, and attached it to my belt. I stuffed the cellular phone and my wallet in my cargo pants pocket. I shut off all unnecessary electronic equipment to limit distractions. Then I checked around the interior to ensure that any loose items were safely stowed.

Tom, who had the joy of trying to drive us through the slowly closing gates of hell, was thoughtful enough to remind me to switch on the remote camera, the chaser's equivalent of an aircraft's black box. I activated the forward-view camera, plugged in the narrator headset and tested, "One … two … three."

The sky between Johnson and Richfield turned a frightening green, and I accepted that there would be no swift escape. The fun of chasing, the jokes and the conversation vanished. We were facing the stark reality of our pursuits. Survival was now the issue. To the east lay a landscape of wheat fields flowing like a white-capped ocean. But this route offered no escape, for the fields were lined with only a handful of tractor access roads that would soon turn to thick mud. Behind us, and to the west, was the storm—bolts of lightning, giant hail stones and the oncoming tornado. No shelter anywhere. Our only escape was due south, where the sun shone pleasantly in the distance.

left: Bright white streaks falling from the side of a storm indicate hail shafts.

right: A blinding dust storm covers the highway near the Kansas and Colorado border.

"Floor it, Tom," I said.

"Already did," he answered.

I continued my narration as the western edge of the storm closed in on us and a light rain began. "Ahhhh … Small problem here—pea- and marble-sized hail on the road. Tom, watch the debris in the road. OK … Tennis-ball-sized stones on the road. Fortunately, we haven't hit anything." The sound of a few small hailstones echoed about. Then, a loud thud, as a big hailstone hit the roof the truck.

"Large hail! Possibly tennis-ball-sized, hitting the truck now," I continued. BANG! A baseball-sized stone crashed into a suction-cup camera mount I had left on the hood, sending it flying, and it now dangled from a safety strap. "One hit to the hood," I stated. No sooner had I uttered the word "hood" than an explosive crack filled the truck, as a couple of stones shattered the front windshield.

"Ahhhh … Direct hit to the windshield. WE'VE LOST IT. Tom, can you see?" I looked over at Tom. He was pale and entirely focused on the road ahead. He shouted, "END! END! END!" The brisk smell of rain-chilled air flowed through the cracks in the window. Another barrage of stones hit, mostly smaller, but a big

one smashed into the right rear quarter-panel window behind me, sounding like a shotgun blast. "We've lost a rear window," I narrated.

The hail slackened off as though Tom's words had been heard by a higher source. I grabbed two thick road atlases and placed them between my chest and the window, expecting the next stone to come right through the fractured glass.

The gauntlet of ice passed and we were clear, except for the tornado looming to the right. I reached for the gaffers tape, always nearby for such emergencies, and taped an "X" on the front windshield to keep it from caving in. When a northbound truck approached, Tom flashed his head lamps, and we both pointed desperately back towards the storm. He waved and kept going. I looked back and watched until brake lights flashed on, and, undoubtedly, he slammed into the wall of ice and rain.

Tom pulled over when we reached Richfield, and we inspected the exterior. I videotaped the damage. There were three large dents, a quarter of an inch deep and two inches wide, on the hood and roof. The front windshield and the right rear panel windows were smashed. Miraculously, the remotely mounted anemometer and plastic wind cups had endured. Another storm chaser whose vehicle had suffered a similar fate stopped alongside. He had not seen John, Marty, or the tornado.

We chased the storm for a short while to the southeast and never found the tornado. I called Amarillo and tried to schedule an appointment with an automotive glass company.

The next day was spent in Amarillo having glass replaced and reorganizing. We didn't know the fate of Marty and John's chase teams until two days later when we met them at another chaser's convergence in west Texas. They had missed the hail.

left: Rock-hard hail stones

top: Hail damage to the Shadow Chaser windshield

No Place Like Home

Chase Log: Monday, March 7, 1994.
Tucson, Arizona.

A late winter afternoon in the desert. I was at my desk, peering out a large picture window at the sky, preparing to work on my chase notes for the approaching season. A few harmless, puffy, white cumulus clouds hovered overhead. No sooner did my fingers touch the keyboard than the phone rang. It was Tom.

"Red alert!" he shouted.

"What?" I asked. Tom rarely overreacted about anything unless he was jesting. "Look west, it's black," he said.

I ran to the top bedroom window and glanced out. Sure enough, a line of dark storm clouds filled the western horizon. I went to my office and turned on the weather radio

Scenic Tucson

as a deep booming roll rattled the windows. OK, I thought, these storms are no big deal, just a typical March rain shower. But just to be safe, I called the computer data service and requested a Doppler radar display from Phoenix.

None too impressive, though there were moderate storms west of Tucson. I returned to the window. The dark clouds seemed to have diminished while moving overhead. The weather radio and the television were not predicting anything special, so I went back to work. Tom's pre-season jitters, I mused.

I chanced to look out once more. This time, I observed a storm base with sloping sides that came together in a small nipple-like protrusion. No way on earth, I thought. It looks like a funnel cloud, but these storms aren't that serious. Besides, I was in Tucson, not Kansas.

I continued to write and kept an eye on the cloud. One more glance, and a small but well-developed funnel cloud, which I had dismissed earlier, was protruding. Its sides vibrated like a snake's belly, up and down along the entire length of the funnel. Off went the computer, into my hands the 35mm camera, and up the stairs I went to my office balcony.

I fired off a few frames, then dialed the Tucson NWS office. Busy signal, time after time. The funnel dropped closer to the ground and continued on a path to my door.

I called Tom and got his answering machine. "Tom, no joking, look southeast; there's a funnel or tornado. It's the real thing!" Then I called Joel and tried to sound less alarmed, for I was aware his wife experienced the catastrophic Topeka, Kansas tornado in 1966 and is understandably terrified of severe weather. Joel wasn't in.

I ran downstairs. Megamouth, my cat, who had been staring at me as I worked the phone, flew by like a bullet for parts unknown. I grabbed my video camera box, ran upstairs and started taping. The vortex now loomed just a few miles away, getting larger and more organized. I reached for the phone again as the funnel

Funnel, and soon-to-be tornado, heading towards Faidley's home in Tucson

cloud's tip appeared to touch the ground. I could see a small debris cloud swirling around the base. It was now a tornado that was making a beeline for my house.

The NWS line was still busy, and no warning had been issued. I called 911. "This is Warren Faidley. I'm an NWS storm spotter," I said. "I'm looking towards the south, and there's a tornado on the ground. I've tried calling the weather service, but I can't get through." "Yes, sir," the operator said. "We're getting numerous reports, but we also get a busy signal."

I was frustrated. A potentially destructive tornado was closing in on my own neighborhood, and I couldn't do a damn thing! I felt for the first time the fear that homeowners in the Plains have for twisters. I wasn't in the Alley chasing a tornado in someone else's backyard. Hell, I was a potential victim!

I was also a journalist, so I squeezed off several more frames as the tornado drew closer. Then, I made one last attempt to call the weather office. Busy.

Just as I was seriously considering the idea of heading to the shelter of a lower-floor closet, the tornado roped out into a long, wispy needle before vaporizing less than a mile from the house. The siren on the weather radio sounded, and a tornado warning was finally broadcast. The winds picked up, and I watched the dark gray, rapidly swirling cloud mass pass directly over the house, half expecting another funnel to drop and yank me off the balcony. ("Mothers of Faidley's childhood playmates to speak at hospital press conference.")

My phone rang, rang and rang. "Hey, I thought that you were kidding," Tom said, half out of breath. "I drove down the street and actually got a few shots." We agreed that a chase was warranted. "I can see some storms between Tucson and Phoenix," he added. "I'm heading that way."

"I'll be right behind you," I said. "But I've got to reassemble the truck." Parts of the interior were in pieces in preparation for the Spring run. Down the steps once again, the phone ringing away in the background. I grabbed the best assortment of gear and headed to Phoenix.

Driving northwest along I-10, I could see a large anvil cloud with an overshooting top, about halfway between Tucson and Phoenix. I grimaced as the dome on top collapsed and then rose again above the solid white anvil. This was a sign of a forming tornado, or "tornadogenesis," in some storms.

I fumbled with the piles of loose wiring trying to get the weather radio to work. Tom had a 40-minute head start. He was my chase partner, but still the competitive juices flowed.

Sixty-five miles northwest of Tucson, I reached the outskirts of Casa Grande. The dark base of the storm, which included a large Texas-style updraft, became visible on the southwest side. I followed the storm to the east, watching as the updraft area went through its usual transformations of organizing, rotating and collapsing. It was an impressive storm that could easily have produced a funnel or tornado at any time.

My mobile phone rang near Coolidge, and it was Joel. He was in Florence, Arizona, to the east. "It sure looks like that big storm wants to do it [tornado]," he said. We agreed to meet in Florence, where the eastern road options ended. Meanwhile, the Shadow Chaser was pelted with marble-sized hail. "Hey, buddy," Joel said. "Sounds like you're back in Kansas!"

The storm reached Florence, and I met up with Joel, who stood suspiciously to one side of a guard tower at the State Prison, staring to the east. We watched the magnificent storm move on, colored by the orange beauty of the setting sun. "Nothing like big game in our own back yard," I said to Joel.

"You got it, brother," he said.

Before I went to bed, I walked onto the patio and looked toward the line of trees where the tornado had loomed. A cool breeze carried the familiar scent of damp creosote trees from across the partially flowing wash. I heard the distant yelp of a coyote. It was peaceful, like so many post-storm evenings.

As I turned to go inside, a spectacular lightning flash illuminated the distant horizon, silhouetting the eastern mountain range against a royal blue glow. I paused for a moment, transfixed by the wonderful, unexpected brilliance.

I was happy to be filled with the same excitement and curiosity that has persisted since my childhood. I looked toward the east and sighed.

I CAN'T WAIT 'TIL SPRING.

Not all weather is bad weather! Rainbow touching the Santa Rita Mountains south of Tucson.

Witch's Brew: A Lay Guide to the Mechanics of Severe Thunderstorms

In order for chaseable or severe storms to form, a number of atmospheric elements must come together in precise timing.

First, there must be an abundant supply of relatively warm, moist air in the lower levels of the atmosphere. Moist air is to a storm what gasoline is to an engine. The amount of moisture is proportional to the *dew point* temperature. (The dew point is the temperature to which the air must be cooled for saturation to occur.) Generally, a surface dew point of 55 degrees Fahrenheit or higher indicates sufficient moisture for the development of severe storms.* Tornado outbreaks, however, are usually associated with dew points above 65 degrees Fahrenheit, because big storms require abundant amounts of free moisture.

**Note that powerful tornadoes have been produced in favorable wind shear environments where the dew points were much lower.*

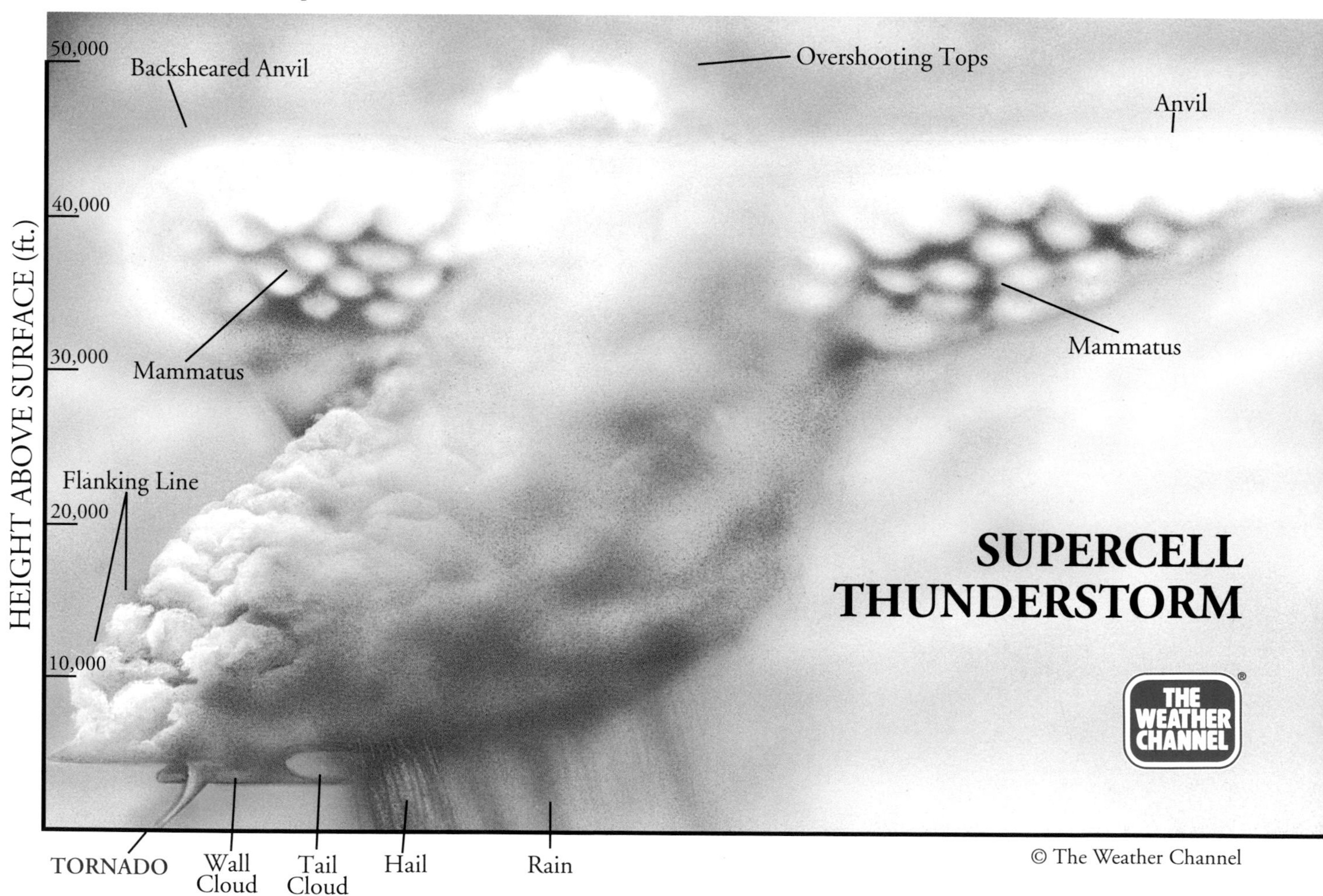

In contrast to the moist air, the air over the desert southwest has extremely low dew points. In certain weather patterns, the dry air moving eastward will set up a *boundary* known as the *dryline.* The contrasting air masses along the dryline, in conjunction with other *dynamics,* can often be a focal point for severe weather. Once the warm, moist air is in place, a series of complicated atmospheric dynamics, *thermodynamics, focusing* and *triggering mechanisms* are necessary to lift the moist air, form a cloud and eventually create a chaseable storm.

Focusing mechanisms are generally localized environmental factors that assist in the *"lifting"* or *"forcing"* of air upward, which can eventually produce a thunderstorm. Examples include: the dryline (the often unstable boundary between moist and dry *air masses*), local topography and *surface heating. Outflow boundaries* created by other storms and the associated wind shear, *convergence* and lifting, can also be local factors.

Another localized feature that can have a profound effect on severe weather is the "*cap.*" The cap, or "lid," is a warm layer of air that is sometimes found above the surface of the earth. It is invisible to the naked eye. If this layer is strong (warm), it may suppress cloud or storm growth completely. On the other hand, if no cap is present, the atmosphere is quite *unstable,* and the wind shear is favorable, storms may explode early in the day, forming into a long line of connected thunderstorm *cells* known as *squall lines.* The storms which make up squall lines can produce all forms of severe weather, but they are generally inefficient tornado producers. Squall lines are also difficult to chase because of their massive, linear structure, which tends to hide low-level storm features.

One of the most dangerous (and chaseable) situations occurs over the Plains when a moderate or strong cap suppresses storm development until a single, or a few, strong *updrafts* overcome it. Once a storm penetrates the cap, it may grow with explosive power and rapidly dominate the atmosphere.

Larger scale lifting or forcing mechanisms can further enhance storm development. Such dynamics are imperative in the development of stronger storms, including *supercells,* which are the most powerful thunderstorms on earth. (Supercells are also the most efficient tornado producers of all thunderstorms.) Lifting mechanisms may include deep fronts (e.g., *cold fronts*), *surface troughs,* or *disturbances* in the upper *troposphere.* These systems are sometimes seen on television *satellite* images as cyclonic *"comma"*-shaped cloud patterns, moving across the country from the west to east. The *surface low pressure,* vertical wind shear and thermodynamic characteristics associated with these fronts can provide a favorable environment for supercell and tornado development.

Once the elements for severe weather are in place, there are a number of mechanisms that can initiate or "trigger" thunderstorm development. The approach of *short-wave disturbances,* low pressure areas, *cold pools* of air in the atmosphere or

Words in italics are further defined in the glossary.

even small-scale, localized lifting events often serve as triggering mechanisms by enhancing the vertical velocity or "lift" in the atmosphere.

The final necessary ingredients in the production of substantial severe storms are *jet streams.* Jet streams are currents of fast-moving air located at various heights in the atmosphere. The flow can travel at speeds of over 150 mph. The jet stream is often made visible by long strands of *cirrus* clouds.

Jet streams, and the dynamics associated with them, serve a number of important functions in creating, moving and sustaining severe storms. As a storm develops, it forms updraft and *downdraft* areas. The downdrafts contain the falling rain, *hail* and/or wind. But it is the persistence of the generally rain-free updraft section(s) that usually determines the life span and severity of a storm. If no jet streams are present, a storm may develop, but it will move little and likely collapse as the updraft is eventually choked by downdraft precipitation. However, if the wind velocity increases sufficiently with height (a component of wind shear commonly referred to as *speed shear*), the updraft will become tilted and hence not choked off by the downdraft. Thus, a favorable jet stream configuration helps a storm move, breathe and stay alive. Supercell storms are most commonly associated with strong or moderate jet streams, in which a main updraft, with upward moving winds of over 100 mph can be maintained for hours. (This also assists in the production of large hailstones.)

The jet streams also play a critical part in creating *directional shear*, an important element in the production of storm rotation *(mesocyclones)* and tornadoes. Directional shear is the gradual turning (or *veering)* of winds from the ground upward. (Generally, clockwise from the SSE to the WNW.) A good way to understand the relationship between directional shear and storm rotation, is to imagine a block of air floating in the sky. If the block encounters favorable shear, it will begin to rotate about a horizontal axis. The same theory can be applied in general to a cloud mass consisting of ice and water.

Favorable shear over the southern Plains is sometimes provided by a combination of two jets: a *low-level jet* stream flowing toward the north-northwest from the Gulf of Mexico, and another upper tropospheric jet flowing from the west, over New Mexico, toward the Mississippi Valley. Favorable shear, especially in the lower levels of the troposphere, may create an internal rotating updraft or mesocyclone within a storm if other necessary elements are present. The exact mechanics that cause a tornado to eventually drop from the storm to the ground are not completely understood. Scientists theorize that a horizontally rolling tube of air along the ground, from downdraft outflows, is tilted and joined with the existing mesocyclone. The rapidly rotating air is then concentrated and made visible either as condensation *funnel* or as a dust or *debris cloud* below the funnel.

Ultimately, it is the precise timing of these elements that determines the severity and types of storms, if any, which form.

Photography Notes

Before embarking upon any attempt to put weather on film, remember two important things:

1. **I do not advocate storm photography for the lay person**. The pursuit and/or photography of severe weather should be left to experienced persons. My notes are intended to supply basic information to those desiring to photograph the gentler side of our atmosphere: clouds, rainbows, sunsets and scenic landscapes.

2. **Any storm is a potential killer.** Even a seemingly innocent storm cloud can produce a single lightning bolt that may be attracted to a metal tripod or your head. Don't forget that flash floods, tornadoes, straight line winds and rock-hard hail stones injure or kill without warning. No one should attempt to chase a storm unless he or she has the proper training and experience.

Cameras:

I do not favor one brand or type of 35mm camera. Most professionals use certain camera brands because of the availability of accessories. Some are simple to use while others require extensive practice. I would advise anyone considering

above: This lightning display was captured just after sunset near Casa Grande, Arizona during the summer monsoon. The exposure was calculated using the small amount of existing light as a starting point. I also closed the aperture one f/stop to compensate for the brilliant lightning. The final exposure was f/5.6 for two minutes, using a 35mm camera, 150mm zoom setting and 50 ISO speed film. No filters were used.

the purchase of equipment to research the brands and consult with an experienced photographer.

Lenses:

When I first started shooting storms, my lenses were short. As I came closer to getting nailed by lightning and tornadoes, my lenses grew like Pinocchio's nose. The reason for this was simple: the longer the lens, the more distance I could place between myself and the danger. Longer lenses are great for shooting clouds and sunsets because they "compress" the subject(s).

Unfortunately, there are drawbacks to longer lenses. They usually have poor light transmission because of the increased amount of internal glass needed for magnification. This, in turn, usually means that the widest f-stop (size of aperture opening) is around f/4.5 to f/5.6. Then again, if you are planning to shoot in bright daylight, or using high speed film, f-stops may not be a problem.

Longer lenses which have f-stops of 2.8 or lower are heavy, bulky and expensive. There are a number of solutions to this dilemma. You can "push" your film (see film notes below) or shoot with shorter lenses and have your pictures enlarged. If you already have longer lenses with limited f-stops, you can use a tripod and increase your exposure time, or simply use a faster film. Another idea is to purchase a teleconverter. This device is mounted between your camera and the lens to increase the focal length. I do not recommend buying a teleconverter unless you purchase a professional model. The optics in inexpensive equipment are terrible and a waste of money. Regardless of the brand, teleconverters cut the amount of light reaching your film, and you will lose a stop or two.

I recommend using zoom lenses. I use a 80-200mm f/2.8 lens that I adore. In fact, with a couple of zooms that cover a range of 28mm to 75mm, and 80-200mm, a photographer has the basic perspectives covered for most shots. In addition, the price of two such zooms may be less than that of buying the six or more fixed focal length lenses to cover the same range. I suggest trying brand-name zooms, as I once had a cheap zoom come apart in my hand. Also, cheaper zooms do not handle heat and cold well.

Film:

I have used film with "speeds" ranging from 25 ISO to 6400 ISO during my endeavors. But I prefer lower speed transparency films such as 50 to 100 ISO for my photography. The lower the ISO number, the slower the film (the less sensitive it is to light) and the longer the exposure. The lower ISO films do have less grain, which is desired by most professionals. On occasion, for more editorial images, which do not demand super sharpness and fine grain, I also use 400 ISO transparency films.

Transparency films are better suited for commercial purposes such as viewing and duplicating. Negative films do have an advantage of having slightly wider latitudes to being over- and under-exposed. A beginner may also want to consider using black-and-white films, which are a great way to learn about exposures, cost less and give wonderful results.

Occasionally I will "push" film. Pushing film allows you to gain exposure ranges by overrating the film's ISO speed and compensating by over-processing the film. All film processors charge an extra fee for this. I suggest experimenting with film types, push speeds and processors before trying this method on a critical shot. If you push film, the entire roll must be shot as pushed at the same rating. You cannot shoot one-half of a roll as pushed. Your film or camera instructions should contain data on pushing film.

Miscellaneous Equipment:

I rarely use filters, with the exception of clear glass filters on the front of my lenses to protect the front element. Filters are, for the most part, creative tools.

As for rain gear, I do not usually shoot in the rain except for hurricane work. Shooting in the rain during thunderstorms is extremely hazardous, and something I never do, because lightning often accompanies the rain shafts.

A handheld exposure meter, as opposed to the in-camera meter, is critical in determining long exposures, especially those involving low light. A cable release is necessary when using a camera mounted on a tripod. This enables the photographer to open and close the shutter without touching the camera.

A tripod is imperative for keeping a camera steady for exposures under 1/60 second. But tripods are hazardous near storms; they're efficient lightning rods.

Special Notes on Lightning:

I'm often asked if I use super-fast film to capture lightning bolts. No. In fact, the slower the film, the better. When I expose for lightning, I usually want to leave the camera's shutter open for a long period of time, allowing the lightning to expose itself. If I used a faster film, my exposure time would be shortened.

Exposures can be complex. I've used exposures ranging from f/8 at 1/250 second to f/2.8 at 30 minutes to expose lightning. The secret is to accurately expose the film for the background, then adjust the overall exposure for the lightning. Calculating the proper exposure depends on the following: the amount of existing daylight, the intensity/frequency of the bolts, the proximity of the camera to the lightning, the type of atmosphere (hazy vs. clear), film type, lens type, movement of the storm, and the residual effects on the film by any existing light source(s).

Happy shooting!

Storm Chase Glossary

This glossary contains the basic explanations of common technical and slang terms which are used in this book or relate to storm chasing and severe weather. Many of the definitions have been simplified.

As it is with all types of scientific terminology, such terms are constantly being redefined, and a few are, by nature, controversial.

Words in *italics* are terms defined elsewhere.

A-bomb: [slang] A thunderstorm or *cumulonimbus tower* which has a mushroom cloud appearance, similar to an atomic bomb cloud.

AC: Anticipated Convective outlook. Same as *convective outlook.*

accessory cloud: A cloud that depends on a larger cloud system, such as a thunderstorm, for its development and existence. *Roll clouds* and *shelf clouds* are two examples.

advection: The horizontal transfer of an atmospheric property, such as temperature or water vapor.

agitated region/area: [slang] An area where groups of *towering cumulus* grow and collapse. Such areas sometimes favor eventual severe storm development.

air mass: A large body of air (generally covering thousands of square miles) which has relatively uniform characteristics of *humidity* and temperature. The boundaries between air masses are called *fronts.*

air mass thunderstorm: Generally, any thunderstorm not associated with strong *dynamics* and/or favorable *wind shear.*

air parcel: An imaginary body of air, a few feet wide, used to visualize the behavior of air. The concept of parcels is often used to estimate atmospheric *soundings.*

air pressure: The amount of force exerted over an area by air molecules. This force, or weight, is called air pressure. The amount of pressure is often measured by a *barometer* in units of inches of mercury, or in millibars. The average sea level pressure is 29.92 inches, while a *hurricane* may have a pressure of 26.55 inches or lower. Rapidly falling air pressures often indicate a *disturbance* is approaching.

altimeter: A *barometer* calibrated to indicate altitude instead of *air pressure.* Altimeters are commonly used in aircraft.

altocumulus (Ac): White or gray clouds, appearing as rounded masses or rolls, occurring in layers or patches, generally located between 6,500 to 15,000 feet. Altocumulus clouds can indicate a *destabilizing* atmosphere.

altocumulus castellanus (ACCAS) (pronounced ACK-kas): Clouds generally located between 6,500 to 15,000 feet. The upper portions of these clouds consist of white *cumulus* clouds, and are taller than they are wide, which gives a turret-shaped appearance. The bases are flat. These clouds may indicate *instability* aloft and the possibility of storm development.

altostratus (As): Grayish clouds generally located between 6,500 to 15,000 feet, in the form of fibrous, striated or uniform sheets or layers. A widespread, thick layer of altostratus may inhibit *surface heating,* which can delay or suppress storm development.

anemometer: An instrument, usually consisting of a staff and three cups that rotate with the wind, that measures wind speed.

anticipated convective outlook: A public forecast issued by the *SPC* several times daily, outlining the area(s) of expected thunderstorms, and the severity of possible storms over the U.S. The potential for severe weather is listed as: *approaching severe, slight risk, moderate risk* or *high risk.* The convective outlook is a popular forecast text amongst storm chasers. Also called AC and convective outlook.

anticyclonic rotation: Clockwise rotation (in the Northern Hemisphere as would be seen from above). The opposite of *cyclonic rotation.*

anticyclonic tornado: A tornadic *vortex* that turns in a clockwise direction (as opposed to tornadoes that turn in a *cyclonic* (counterclockwise) direction). Less than 1% of all Northern Hemisphere tornadoes are anticyclonic.

anvil cloud: The upper portion of a thunderstorm, often shaped like a blacksmith's anvil, consisting mainly of ice crystals. Anvils may spread out for hundreds of miles from the main storm as *jet stream* winds carry the clouds downwind. A solid, intact anvil cloud, with *backshearing,* is usually indicative of a strong storm. The *overshooting tops* or *domes* of anvils may reach above 60,000 feet.

anvil crawlers: [slang-Rhoden] Lightning bolts which spread out underneath a storm's *anvil.*

anvil rings: [slang] Circular rings or cloud *striations* sometimes associated with an *anvil* cloud. Also called "Saturn rings."

anvil rollover: [slang] A circular or semicircular lip of clouds which occurs along the underside of a *back-sheared anvil.*

approaching severe: A thunderstorm with winds of 40 to 57 mph, or hail 1/2 to 3/4 inches in diameter.

arcing (flashes): The bright white, blue or green flashes associated with powerlines and/or transformers being hit by a tornado, hurricane or strong winds. Spotters often look for arcing at night as an indication of tornadoes or destructive winds.

ARES: Amateur Radio Emergency Service. A group of amateur *ham* radio operators who assist in relaying severe weather information. [Also see *spotter net.*, and *storm spotter.*]

ASOS: Automated Surface Observation System. An unmanned weather station which relays data via computer.

backing winds: Generally, winds which shift in a counterclockwise direction over a period of time at a given location. Chasers often watch *surface plots* for backing winds that change from south to southeasterly at the surface. This change in the direction of the winds may increase *dew points,* but more importantly, often create favorable *veering* with height of low-level winds.

backsheared anvil: [slang] A thunderstorm *anvil* which spreads upwind, against the prevailing winds aloft. A backsheared anvil indicates strong anvil-level *divergence* and intense *updrafting.* Generally associated with severe storms.

back-door cold front: A *cold front* that advances in a more east-to-west manner as opposed to the more common west-to-east or north-to-south direction.

ball lightning: See *lightning.*

barber pole: [slang] A vertical storm *tower* having the appearance of being twisted like a barber's pole. This type of structure is usually indicative of a strong, rotating *updraft.*

barometer: An instrument used to measure *air pressure.*

barometric pressure: Same as *air pressure.*

bead lightning: See *lightning.*

bear's cage: [slang] A dangerous region of a thunderstorm where *storm-scale* rotation is obscured by heavy *precipitation.* The term is often used to describe the hazard of chasing in such an area. [Also see *core punch* and *mesocyclone.*]

beauty light: The flat, soft light that occurs shortly before or after sunset or sunrise. This light, or glow, is favored by photographers for its golden, warm tones and lack of harsh contrast.

beaver tail: [slang] A low, flat cloud often shaped like a beaver's tail, located near the *inflow* region of a thunderstorm.

blue box: [slang] A severe thunderstorm *watch* box. Also called "blue watch."

blue jet: See *lightning.*

"bolt from the blue": See *lightning.*

bomb: 1. Any explosively developing thunderstorm or *cyclone.* 2. An intense, rapidly developing storm over the ocean, especially in the North Atlantic and North Pacific Oceans.

boundary layer: Generally, a layer of air residing in the lowest one-half mile of the atmosphere. It is within this area that winds *(such as the LLJ)* are affected by friction with the earth's surface and temperatures are most strongly affected by daytime insolation and nighttime radiational cooling.

bow echo: A radar term used to describe a bow-shaped line of thunderstorm *cells.* Bow echoes often produce strong and damaging *straight-line winds.*

box: [slang] A geographical area of the United States outlined for the possibility of severe weather. Boxes are issued for tornado and severe thunderstorm *watches.* Also called "watch box."

bubble high: Same as *mesohigh.*

bust: [slang] An inaccurate forecast or an unsuccessful storm chase. This term also refers to situations in which severe weather is expected but does not occur.

CA: See Cloud-to-Air *lightning.*

cap: A layer of warm air sometimes found around 4,000 to 12,000 feet above the surface. The cap, or "capping inversion," can completely suppress or delay thunderstorm development by preventing *parcels* of air from rising. A favorable chase scenario occurs when the atmosphere is *unstable* and a strong, but breakable cap inhibits widespread storm development until a strong *cumulonimbus tower* "breaks the cap," rapidly developing into a *supercell*(s) which dominates the atmosphere. [Also see *loaded gun.*]

CAPE: See *Convective Available Potential Energy.*

carousel event: [slang] A rare tornadic event where two or more separate tornadoes revolve around each other in a carousel-type fashion, usually from a large *mesocyclone.* The tornadoes from a carousel event are sometimes referred to as *satellites.*

Cb: See *Cumulonimbus* cloud.

CB: Citizens Band radio (26.965 MHz to 27.405 MHz). A radio system used extensively by truckers and some chasers to relay information and cross-talk. Due to the lack of transmitting power (usually less than three miles), CB radio is not considered a reliable form of communication. [Also see *ham* radio.]

CC: See Cloud-to-Cloud lightning. [Also see *lightning*.]

cell: Convection in the form of a single updraft, downdraft, or updraft/downdraft couplet. For example, a *towering cumulus* cloud or *precipitation* shaft. The term is also used figuratively to describe a storm *echo* on radar. A typical thunderstorm consists of multiple cells. [Also see *supercell, multicell, multi-line, mature stage* and *single cell.*]

CG: Cloud-to-Ground lightning. Made up of negative and positive charges. [Also see *lightning*.]

chaos theory: The theory that weather (and other natural systems) are ultimately unpredictable, because initial conditions can never be perfectly specified.

chase distance/time compression: The phenomenon that sometimes occurs after years of chasing over the same highways, where the time involved with extremely long distance driving seems to become compressed. Such compression can make long journeys tolerable.

chase fever: [slang] The anxious, excited feeling that most hard-core chasers have as the spring chase season approaches.

chase groupie: [slang] A person who is obsessed with severe weather, storm chasing and/or chasers. Generally, a chase groupie does not actually chase. Groupies are not necessarily obsessed in a negative manner. Some are people who are afraid to chase, while others are unable to chase because of physical or economic reasons.

chase season(s): The primary periods for chasing severe weather. Tornadoes: April 15 through June 15 in the Plains. Lightning: July 7 through September 15 in the desert southwest. Hurricanes: August 15 through October 15 in the Gulf and east coast regions.

chase whore: [slang] A person or company who abuses or misuses a chaser's video footage, photographs, etc., i.e., offering unfair reproduction rights or committing copyright infringement.

chaser convergence: [slang] The unplanned meeting (convergence) of storm chasers, that usually occurs toward the end of the chase day, in the vicinity of the most promising storms.

chaser vertigo/fatigue: [slang] A sometimes dangerous condition most commonly caused by fatigue, dehydration or low blood sugar. Chaser vertigo may include disorientation, viewing of mirages such as pseudo storm *towers* on the horizon or ghost vehicles in the passing lane.

chaser's caravan: [slang] A group of four or more chase vehicles actively engaged in intercepting a storm. "Caravanning" is generally frowned upon by experienced chasers, because it can generate an appearance of revelry.

chaser's flack: [slang-Faidley] *Hailstones.* [Also see *souvenirs.*]

chaser's neck: [slang-Faidley] A sore, stiff neck caused by excessive head turning while chasing storms.

chaser's penalty: [slang-Moller] The price, i.e., time, money, frustration, that a chaser pays for traveling hundreds of miles without seeing a storm because of an inaccurate forecast or inexperience.

chaser's withdrawal: [slang] A depressed feeling chasers develop during the off-season, especially the winter.

CHQ: [slang-Faidley] Chasers Headquarters. A motel, apartment or other building used as a temporary chase operations center while traveling away from home.

Chubasco: A Spanish term used for any brief, heavy rainstorm or thunderstorm.

cirrus (Ci): High clouds consisting of ice crystals, found at altitudes of 16,000 feet or higher. Cirrus clouds often appear as white feathery streaks, or narrow white bands or patches. Thunderstorm *anvils* are a form of cirrus. A widespread, thick layer of cirrus may inhibit *surface heating*, which can delay or suppress storm development.

cirrus streak: A narrow *cirrus* cloud band associated with a *jet stream* or *jet streak.*

classic supercell: A type of *supercell* storm. A supercell with a *precipitation*-free region of rotation and heavy *precipitation* in the *forward-flank.* Most chasers prefer this type of storm, because tornadoes are generally produced from a precipitation-free, *wall cloud* area, as opposed to *high-precipitation supercells.* [Compare with *high-precipitation* and *low-precipitation* supercells.]

clear slot: An area of clearing skies or cloud cover, often indicating an intrusion of drier air, applying to either *storm-scale* or *synoptic-scale* features. On the storm-scale, clear slots are often seen as clearing cloud material near the southern region of an occluding *updraft.*

closed eye wall: A well-structured *hurricane eye wall* with no gaps or deformities. A closed eye wall may denote a strong or strengthening storm. [Compare with *open eye wall.*]

closed low: A *low pressure* area completely circled by *isobars.* [Compare with *open trough.*]

Cloud Stalker ™ : Warren Faidley's chase nickname.

cloud tags: See *fractus* clouds.

cold air advection: The transport of cold air into a region by horizontal winds. Such advection aloft can assist in *destabilization.*

cold air funnel: A *funnel cloud* or usually weak *tornado* that forms from a thunderstorm, rain shower or *cumulus* cloud in environments where the air aloft is unusually cold or in rain-cooled air.

cold front: A zone where a cold *air mass* advances and replaces a warm air mass. Storms may form along or slightly ahead of the boundary, due to the increased *instability* caused by layer *lifting* associated with the front.

cold pool: *Synoptic-scale:* An area of cold air in the mid-*troposphere* that can increase *instability. Storm-scale:* a *precipitation*-cooled area left in the wake of a thunderstorm, which can inhibit further storm development.

collar cloud: A circular cloud ring which often surrounds the upper part of a *wall cloud.*

Colorado low: A surface *low pressure* area which forms over the eastern slopes of the Rocky Mountains. Such lows enhance the severe weather potential in the Plains if other *elements* are present.

comma cloud: A *synoptic-scale,* comma-shaped cloud pattern. Comma clouds are often seen on *satellite* images in association with *low pressure* systems, or *cyclones.*

comma echo: A radar term used to describe the comma-shaped top portion of a *bow echo.*

convection: The vertical transport of *moisture* and heat by updrafts and downdrafts, sometimes as thunderstorms but most commonly as convection currents.

convective available potential energy (CAPE): A measure of the amount of energy available for *convection.* The CAPE is directly related to the maximum potential vertical speed within an *updraft.* Higher values may indicate a greater potential for severe weather. CAPE is measured from *thermodynamic* profiles of the atmosphere called *soundings.*

convective outlook: See *anticipated convective outlook.*

convective temperature: The approximate temperature to which surface air must be warmed in order to eliminate the stable surface layer. [See *cap.*]

convergence: A directional merging or piling up of winds that can result in upward forcing, assisting in storm development.

core: The area of a thunderstorm, usually located in the *forward-* or *rear-flank downdrafts,* which contains the heaviest rain and the largest *hail.* Also refers to the center of a tornadic *vortex.*

core punching, plunge: [slang] A penetration by a vehicle into the *core* of a storm. Core punching is an extremely dangerous maneuver that places the chaser in the heaviest *precipitation* (rain and large hail) areas of the storm. Core punching is also hazardous because tornadoes can be embedded in, or around, the core.

Coriolis Effect: The effect caused by the rotation of the earth that deflects any free moving object (such as wind) to the right of its path in the Northern Hemisphere. The deflection is greater the faster the wind motion and the longer the *air parcel* is in motion. This effect is significant at the larger scales but has been shown to be relatively unimportant in *tornadogenesis.*

corkscrew: [slang] A term used to describe the twisting motion in a convective *tower,* often seen as cloud *striations* or a *barber pole* effect. Implies rotation within the storm.

crepuscular rays: Shafts or beams of light sometimes seen when the sun moves behind clouds, especially at sunset. Also called "Jesus rays."

CS: [slang-Faidley] Cloud-to-structure lightning. [Also see *lightning.*]

Cu: *Cumulus* cloud.

cumulonimbus (Cb): A cloud, associated with thunderstorms, characterized by a strong vertical development in the form of huge, cauliflower-like *towering* clouds, usually topped by an *anvil* cloud. Also called thunderhead.

cumulus (Cu): Detached, low-level clouds, generally found at less than 6,000 feet, often appearing as mounds or domes with sharp outlines. [Also see *towering cumulus.*]

cumulus field: A large area of *cumulus* clouds. Chasers will often watch these areas of vertical cloud growth for the development of storms. A significant cumulus field within a *capped* region is often a sign that the *cap* may be ready to break.

curtains: Veils, streaks or heavy shafts of falling rain and/or *hail.*

cutoff low: A closed area of *low pressure* aloft that has become completely detached from the main, westerly wind flow.

cyclic storm: A thunderstorm that goes through cycles of intensification and weakening while maintaining its individuality. Many *supercells* are cyclic, which allows them to produce multiple tornadoes. A thunderstorm that undergoes only a single cycle is called a *pulse storm.*

cyclogenesis: The process by which a new *cyclone* is created, or the process that causes the intensification of a pre-existing cyclone.

cyclone: Any *low pressure* area associated with winds circulating counterclockwise (in the Northern Hemisphere as seen from above). The two main types of cyclones are *extratropical* and *tropical.* The term cyclone was once used to describe *tornadoes.*

cyclonic rotation: Rotation in a counterclockwise direction (in the Northern Hemisphere as seen from above). The opposite of *anticyclonic rotation.*

danger zone: [slang] A particularly dangerous region of a thunderstorm, e.g., near the *core, bear's cage, wall cloud,* or in a highly electrically charged storm area.

dBz: See *echo.*

death ridge: A large, strong area of *high pressure* which prevents severe weather and, thus, chasing. Also called "ridged out."

death sky: [slang-Faidley] The phenomenon of skies turning a weird green or yellowish hue before some severe storms, hail storms and tornadoes. Caused in part by the scattering of light through storm clouds and heavy *precipitation.* Also called "green sky."

debris cloud: A <u>rotating</u> cloud of dust or debris, near the ground, that often appears beneath a condensation *funnel* or surrounding the base of a *tornado.* Many tornadoes begin as a debris or *dust whirl* on the ground, underneath the *wall cloud.* Special note: A <u>rotating</u> debris cloud seen underneath the base of a storm *updraft,* or under a funnel cloud, usually constitutes storm-to-ground circulation and a confirmed tornado.

debris zone: [slang] An area where debris from a tornado is either falling or has already fallen.

deep strike: [slang-Marshall] A chase of 500 or more miles in a single day.

Denver cyclone: Surface *convergence* partially forced by local topography, which occurs near Denver. This can often act as a *focusing mechanism* for severe weather.

derecho (Pronounced day-RAY-cho. Spanish for "straight"): A widespread, usually fast moving, and often violent, *straight-line* windstorm created by groups of strong thunderstorms.

destabilization: The tendency for a stabilized environment to become *unstable* because of large scale factors (e.g., destabilization due to dynamic *lift)* and/or smaller scale factors (e.g., *mesoscale moisture convergence* or local heating leading to destabilization). Opposite of *stabilized.*

dew point (Td): A measurement of atmospheric *moisture.* The temperature to which air must be cooled at a given *pressure* in order for saturation and subsequent condensation to occur. At a given pressure, the dew point temperature is directly related to the amount of water vapor present. Dew points above 55 degrees Fahrenheit are generally high enough to support severe weather.

directional shear: The component of *wind shear* which is due to a change in wind <u>direction</u> with height, e.g., southeasterly winds at the surface and southwesterly winds aloft. Favorable directional shear (or veering), in combination with *speed shear* in the low levels of the *troposphere,* is important in the development of *mesocyclones* and in augmenting *updraft* strength. [Also see *helicity.*]

dissipating stage: The last stage in a thunderstorm's *life cycle.*

disturbance: A term used to describe any deviation in flow or pressure that is associated with, causes or intensifies cloudiness or *precipitation.* Typically, the term refers to *synoptic-scale* cyclonic circulations, e.g., *long wave* and *short wave troughs,* but may also refer to other phenomena such as *jet streaks.*

divergence: The expansion or spreading out of a vector field, e.g., winds. Divergence in the upper *troposphere* enhances upward motion and can increase the potential for severe weather development, if other necessary *elements* are present.

dome: Same as *overshooting top.*

Doppler radar (Also called WSR-88D, or <u>W</u>eather <u>S</u>urveillance <u>R</u>adar 19<u>88-D</u>.): A highly sensitive radar that can measure the radial velocity of objects moving toward or away from the radar, including rotation (*mesocyclones*) within storms. Doppler radar can also measure *echo* intensity, i.e., *precipitation* levels and many other parameters. Although Doppler radar can detect rotation, it cannot confirm an actual tornadic circulation on the ground. (Spotters are still needed for this.) Doppler radar is part of the *NEXRAD* program. The WSR-88D replaced the older WSR-57 and 74C radar systems.

downburst: A strong *downdraft* resulting in an outward burst of damaging winds on or near the ground. Wind speeds near the ground from a strong downburst can exceed 100 mph. [Also see *microburst.*]

down day: [slang] A non-chase day during the chase season.

downdraft: The area(s) of a storm where air and/or *precipitation* is falling. [Also see *wind shear.*]

drop: [slang] A tornado "dropping" to the ground.

dryline: A boundary that separates moist and dry *air masses.* It typically lies on a north-south line during the spring storm season, and separates the Gulf *moisture* to the east and the dry desert air toward the west. It is along or just to the east of this line that severe storms often initially develop, due in part to the *instability* of the contrasting air masses. The dryline is a major focusing point for chasers. (It is also the author's favorite area to chase.)

dryline bulge: A bulge in the *dryline,* which usually represents an area where the dry air is locally advancing eastward near the surface faster than it is further north and south. The area north of the bulge (in the moist air) may create a local focus for severe weather.

dryline storm/supercell: Generally, any thunderstorm that forms along the dryline. [Also see *low-precipitation supercells.*]

dry microburst: A *microburst* with little or no precipitation, often appearing as a *dust foot.*

dry punch/slot: A band of dry air residing over a moist layer or a band of dry air that wraps cyclonically around the east side of a *low pressure system.* If other *elements* are present, such drier air can increase *instability.*

dust devil: A small and usually harmless *vortex* made visible by dust or debris, which forms in response to surface heating during hot, fair weather. On rare occasions, strong dust devils have caused aircraft accidents and structural damage to unreinforced or unsecured property.

dust foot: A sometimes fast-moving cloud of dust which extends outward near the ground, caused by a *downburst* or *microburst.*

dust front: [slang-Faidley] The leading edge of a dust storm, often appearing as a wedge-shaped cloud of turbulent dust.

dust plume: An area of disturbed dust associated with a thunderstorm, which does not rotate, e.g., a *dust foot.* [Compare with *dust whirl.*]

dust storm: A large plume of dust created by *downburst* winds. Intense dust storms occasionally form in the desert southwest when the *outflow boundaries* from storms merge to create a thick, blinding wall of dust.

dust whirl: 1. A rotating column of dust in contact with the ground below a *funnel* or *wall cloud* created by tornadic circulation. (Many tornadoes begin as dust whirls.) 2. A dust whirl caused by non-tornadic circulation, e.g., a dust devil.

dynamics: 1. Large-scale *lifting mechanisms* associated with *synoptic-scale* and larger features that can assist in the development of severe weather. The vertical motions associated with *short wave* disturbances and *jet streaks* in the middle and upper *troposphere* are often treated synonymously with this term. 2. *Storm-scale* lifting mechanisms associated with vertical shear and rotation that can augment the buoyant *updraft* and assist in the development of deep *convection.* Such mechanisms have been shown to be important in the development of *supercells.*

dynamic system: A *long wave trough* with embedded *short waves.* Dynamic storm systems *lift* large portions of the atmosphere and increase severe weather potential if other necessary *elements* are present.

EAS: See *Emergency Alert System.*

EBS: See *Emergency Broadcast System.*

echo: A radar term for the energy reflected by an object, such as the *precipitation* particles in a storm. The level of reflected energy is measured in decibels (dBz). [Also see *Doppler radar.*]

eddy: 1. Ground eddy. [slang] Any number of weak, non-tornadic circulations in contact with the ground. They are often caused by thermals (*dust devils*), small-scale surface wind *convergence* or man-made turbulence. 2. Eddies associated with non-tornadic cloud features, e.g., under the leading edge of a *shelf cloud.* 3. Eddies within a hurricane *eye wall.* [Also see *dust whirl.*]

elements: [slang] Figuratively, any number of meteorological factors that assist in the creation of severe weather, including, but not limited to: *thermodynamics, jet streams,* favorable *wind shear, orographics,* and *lifting mechanisms.*

El Niño: The name given to the warming of the Pacific Ocean from around the International Date Line to the coast of Peru. This small rise in temperature is theorized to cause major changes in the weather patterns affecting the U.S. The overall effect of the El Niño on the Plains' tornado season is still debatable.

Emergency Alert System (EAS): An emergency notification system which alerts the public to dangerous weather and other emergencies via the AM/FM radio, selected cable systems and television. The new EAS is scheduled to replace the *EBS* in 1996.

Emergency Broadcast System (EBS): The EBS system, including the high-pitched tone (most often heard during tests), is activated on television and radio to inform the public of emergencies including severe weather. The EBS is scheduled to be replaced by the *EAS* in 1996.

enhanced wording: A text option used in some tornado and severe thunderstorm *watches* when the potential for strong-to-violent tornadoes, or other forms of severe weather, is considered high. [Also see *PDS.*]

enhanced V: The V-shaped pattern observed on the *anvil* tops of some severe thunderstorms, as seen on infrared *satellite* imagery.

entrance region: A region within a *jet streak* where the wind enters generally from the west. The portion of the entrance region south of the jet axis is called the "right rear quadrant region" or "right entrance region" and is associated with strong upper *tropospheric divergence,* mid-tropospheric upward motion and strong surface *pressure* falls. This area may also serve as a *trigger.* [Also see *exit region.*]

exit region: A region within a *jet streak* where the wind exits downstream (generally toward the east.) The portion of the exit region north of the jet axis is called the "left front quadrant" or "left exit region." This area is associated with upper *tropospheric divergence,* mid-tropospheric upward motion and surface *pressure* falls. The *lifting* associated with this area may also serve as a *trigger* for *convection* by providing a source of *destabilization.* [Also see *entrance region.*]

extratropical cyclone: A *cyclone* that forms outside the tropics, or a tropical cyclone that has lost its tropical characteristics. [Compare to *tropical cyclone.*]

eye: The center of a storm, generally associated with *hurricanes.*

eye wall: The circle of intense thunderstorms that separate the hurricanes *eye* and the *feeder* or *spiral bands.* Strong *vortices* may occur within the eye wall, causing additional destruction.

F5: The highest numerical rating for a tornado or a hurricane. [Also see *Fujita Scale* and the *Saffir-Simpson Hurricane Damage Potential Scale.*]

F-Scale: See *Fujita Scale.*

favorable shear: See *wind shear.*

feeder band(s): Lines of low-level clouds that move (feed) into a thunderstorm or a hurricane. [Also see *spiral bands.*]

fist of God: [slang] 1. An impressive *cumulonimbus tower* with an *overshooting top.* (This feature usually implies a moderately or highly unstable atmosphere with favorable *wind shear.*) 2. Term is also used to describe any impressive, elongated storm tower.

flack (chaser's flack): [slang-Faidley] *Hailstones,* especially those which hit a chase vehicle.

flanking line: A line of *towering cumulus* clouds connecting to, and extending outward from, the most active part of the storm, usually the rear west/southwest region. This line of clouds can have the appearance of *stair-stepping* or feeding into the main body of a *supercell.*

flash flood: A sudden torrent of flood waters usually associated with a thunderstorm. Flash floods kill an average of 140 people each year. The majority of deaths occur when people try to cross flooded roadways in cars.

flashes: See *arcing.*

flying saucer: [slang] A circular, low-level cloud feature shaped like a flying saucer or a stack of *plates.* Usually associated with the rotating *wall cloud* of an *LP supercell.*

focusing mechanism: Localized *lifting* and *destabilization* which can assist in storm development. The *dryline,* surface heating, *upslope* and *outflow boundaries* are common examples. [Related to *forcing* and *triggering mechanisms.*]

fognado: [slang] See *streamnado.*

forcing: Any number of mechanisms which cause or assist in the upward forcing or *lifting* of: 1. a small *parcel* of air, e.g., forcing caused by *outflow boundaries,* or local topography. 2. Large-scale forcing, e.g., caused by the *dynamics* associated with *troughs.* [Related to *triggering mechanisms* and *focusing mechanisms.*]

forward-flank downdraft (FFD): The region of *downdraft* in the downwind part of a *supercell.* This area contains the heaviest *precipitation.*

fractus: Ragged appearing cloud fragments that are not attached to a larger cloud base. Also called "scud" and "cloud tags." Fractus clouds are often seen in the vicinity of, and are sometimes drawn into, a strong *updraft* or *wall cloud.*

front: Including *cold,* warm, occluded and stationary fronts. Fronts are transitional zones between *air masses.* Storms may form along, behind or ahead of these fronts. *Cold fronts* are generally the most active of the three types.

frontogenesis: The formation of a *front.*

Fujita Scale: Developed by Dr. Theodore Fujita, a renowned severe weather researcher at the University of Chicago. This scale rates tornado intensity by post-tornado damage survey information.

F0 Gale tornado (40-72 mph): Light damage. Small branches broken off trees; damage to sign boards. Of the total number of reported tornadoes, about 29% are F0's. (Figures rounded off.)

F1 Moderate tornado (73-112 mph): Moderate damage. Surfaces peeled off roofs; mobile homes pushed off bases; moving autos pushed off the road. Represents 40% of tornadoes.

F2 Significant tornado (113-157 mph): Considerable damage. Roofs torn off frame houses; mobile homes demolished; boxcars pushed over. Represents 24% of tornadoes.

F3 Severe tornado (158-206 mph): Severe damage. Roofs and some walls torn off well-constructed houses; trains overturned; heavy cars lifted off the ground and thrown. Represents 6% of tornadoes.

F4 Devastating tornado (207-260 mph): Devastating damage. Well-constructed houses leveled; structures with weak foundations blown distances. Represents 2% of tornadoes.

F5 Incredible tornado (261-318 mph): Rare. Incredible damage. Strong frame houses lifted off foundations and carried considerable distances to disintegrate; automobile-sized missiles hurled in excess of 100 mph. Represents less than 1% of tornadoes.

F6 to F12 Super tornado (319 mph to Mach 1): This is a theoretical rating, as the maximum winds of a tornado are not expected to reach an F6 speed.

funnel cloud: A condensation cloud appearing in a classic funnel or rope shape that extends from the base of the storm, associated with a rotating column of air, that is not in contact with the ground. If the funnel cloud touches the ground, either as a complete condensation cloud or as a visual *dust whirl* or *debris cloud* beneath the cloud, it then officially becomes a *tornado.* Small funnels are sometimes seen around the base or sides of *cumulus* or *cumulonimbus* clouds. These harmless funnels are caused by localized *wind shear.* [Also see *cold air funnel* and *tornado/funnel shape names.*]

garden variety storm: [slang] Any non-severe storm.

geostationary orbiting earth satellite (GOES): A weather satellite in a fixed position, approximately 22,000 miles above the equator.

glaciated: A term often used to describe fuzzy appearing *anvil* clouds or *towers,* usually denoting weak *updrafts.*

GOES: See *geostationary orbiting earth satellite.*

great wall (of chasing): [slang-Faidley] Interstate 35 in central Oklahoma, which (in general) divides the flat, chaseable terrain toward the west from the visibility-limiting foliage and hilly terrain to the east. [Also see *hotzone.*]

green flash: [slang] See *arcing.* (Note: Term commonly refers to an optical phenomenon that occurs during sunset.)

green sky: [slang] Same as *death sky.*

gust front: The leading edge of the thunderstorm's *downdraft* air. Gust fronts can appear as ground hugging, wedge-shaped clouds (also called a *shelf cloud.*) Gust fronts form as cold air falls from the upper regions of the storm and the air condenses as it spreads out ahead of the storm. Although gust fronts sometimes appear incredibly menacing, they do not generally produce deadly weather. [Also see *gustnado.*]

gustnado: [slang] A small tornado that occurs along the *gust front.* These usually weak and short-lived *vortices* are most commonly seen as *dust whirls* on the ground.

hailbow: [slang] A rainbow caused by a *hailshaft.*

hail curtain: Also called "hail streak" and "curtains." Shafts or veils of hail usually appearing as white streaks.

hailfog: Fog (condensation) caused by large amounts of *hail* on the ground. Occasionally, hailfog can be so intense that it produces zero-visibility.

hailroar: A roaring sound produced by some severe storms caused by the collision of hail stones. (Not to be confused with constant *thunder.*)

hailstone: Balls or clumps of ice that form as supercooled rain drops are frozen and re-frozen as the stone travels up and down in a storm's strong updraft. Hailstones cause over an estimated $800 million in damages each year, including the destruction of crops. The world's largest hailstone on record fell on Coffeyville, Kansas, on September 3, 1970. It weighed 1.67 pounds and was 5.5 inches in diameter. Only two deaths have been reported in the U.S. from hailstones. But in northern India, 246 people were killed by a hailstorm in 1888.

Hailstone sizes. (Official NWS listings in inches.)

Pea	0.25	
Penny	0.75	(falls at around 35 mph)
Quarter	1.00	

Half Dollar	1.25	
Golf ball	1.75	(falls at around 55 mph)
Tennis Ball	2.50	
Baseball	2.75	
Grapefruit	4.00	(also called softball) (falls at around 100 mph)

hailswath: The area or path where hail has fallen. [Also see *white harvest.*]

halo: A narrow whitish or opalescent ring centered around the sun (or moon), usually associated with a layer of thin *cirrus* clouds. Halos are caused by the refraction of light through ice crystals in the clouds.

ham radio: An FCC-licensed amateur radio system used by many *spotters* and some chasers, for cross-talk and to relay important weather-related information. (144.00-148.00 MHz and 440.00-450.00 MHz are the most popular frequency ranges.) [Also see *Skywarn, spotter net.,* and *storm spotter.*]

heat lightning: See *lightning.*

helicity: In chasing: the measurement of the tendency for helical (e.g., corkscrew-spin) motion to occur in horizontal air streams. A mesocyclone may develop when helicity in the horizontal flow is tilted vertically by a thunderstorm's *updraft.* Helicity is proportional to the following: the strength of the horizontal wind flow and the amount of vertical *wind shear* in the flow. Helicity is calculated from the vertical wind profile (a *hodograph)* of the lowest 1 to 2 miles of the atmosphere as obtained by an *atmospheric sounding.* Higher numerical values of helicity (over 150) may favor the formation of low-level storm rotation, or *mesocyclones* in thunderstorm *updrafts.*

high base storm: A storm with a base of more than 3,000 feet above the ground. Such storms are common in the Plains and southwestern U.S. during the summer *monsoon.*

high-precipitation supercell (HP): A type of *supercell* storm. Characterized by high levels of *precipitation,* which often envelop the *forward* and *rear flank downdrafts,* masking areas of rotation. Thus, HPs are difficult and dangerous to chase because of poor visibility and the occurrence of possible *satellite tornadoes.* [Compare with *low-precipitation* and *classic supercells.*]

high pressure: An area of the atmosphere where the *air pressure* is noticeably higher than that of the surrounding areas. (Seen as an "H" on weather maps.) The air around a high pressure area turns in a clockwise direction. The sinking air associated with the center of high pressure generally brings fair weather.

high risk (of severe weather): A forecast issued by the *Severe Local Storms Unit* (SELS) in the *convective outlook.* A high risk is noted when severe weather is expected to affect ten percent or more of an outlined area. A high risk probability occurs only a handful of times per year, and implies a dangerous situation with the possibility of an outbreak of severe weather and tornadoes. [Also see *slight risk, moderate risk* and *PDS.*]

hobbyist (chasers): Responsible people who chase storms as a hobby. The majority of chasers are hobbyists. Many hobbyist chasers also serve as *spotters.* Some hobbyist chasers have occupations, educational pursuits or professions that relate to severe weather, but their main income is not derived from storm chasing. Also called weekend warriors. [Also see *media, professional, outlaw, scientific chasers* and *spotters.]*

hodograph: A graphical representation of the vertical change in the horizontal wind field. A clockwise change in the wind direction with height is often associated with severe thunderstorms. A hodograph curved in a clockwise sense *(directional shear)* and with strong *speed shear* is often associated with *supercell* storms. [Also see *helicity.*]

holiday factor: [slang] A chaser term used to describe the (bogus) increased severe weather potential on holidays. Although outbreaks have occurred on holidays (e.g., the Easter Sunday outbreak of 1913 which killed 94 in Omaha), there is no factual basis for this theory.

hook echo: A radar term used to describe a reflectivity *signature* characterized by a hook-shaped extension of a thunderstorm *echo,* usually in the southwestern sector of the storm. A hook is often associated with a *mesocyclone* and indicates favorable conditions for a tornado, although many tornadoes form without a hook echo and not all hook echoes are associated with tornadoes.

hot zone: [slang-Faidley] High occurrence of tornadoes zone. An area within Tornado Alley which has the highest occurrence of chaseable tornadic activity.

HP supercell: See *high-precipitation supercell.*

humidity: A measure of the air's water vapor content.

hurricane (HUR): A severe *tropical cyclone* with maximum sustained winds of 74 mph or more, occurring in the Atlantic or eastern Pacific Oceans. Although the damaging winds in a hurricane can be sustained at over 150 mph, the greatest danger from hurricanes is the storm surge that can reach over 20 feet. Hurricanes are incredibly powerful storms; just one percent of the energy in an average hurricane could meet the entire energy needs of the U.S. for a full year. The force of the winds near the eye of a hurricane is equivalent to an atomic bomb exploding every ten seconds! [Also see *Saffir-Simpson Hurricane Damage Potential Scale.*]

hurricane warning: A warning is issued when winds of 74+ mph are expected over a specific coastal area within 24 hours.

hurricane watch: A statement that is issued to specific coastal areas when a Hurricane poses a possible threat, usually within 36 hours.

hybrid storm/supercell: Any storm that does not fit into a specific category. Many *supercell* storms are hybrids.

hygrometer: An instrument used for measuring the relative *humidity.*

hypercane: A theoretical supersonic hurricane of immense size and power, caused by an undersea volcano which heats the ocean to over 122 degrees Fahrenheit.

inflow, inflow jet: Winds that flow into a storm, *vortex* or other circulation. Inflow most commonly refers to the warm, moist, southerly low-level winds that flow into the base of a thunderstorm.

inflow stinger: [slang] A *beaver tail* cloud with a stinger-like shape.

instability: The tendency for air parcels to accelerate upward after being *lifted.* The greater the instability, the higher the chances for severe weather. [Also see *lifted index.*]

inversion: See *cap.*

isobar: A line on a weather map connecting points of equal *air pressure.*

isohume: A line on a weather map connecting points of equal *humidity.*

isotherm: A line on a weather map connecting points of equal temperature.

Jesus rays: [slang] Same as *crepuscular rays.*

jet max/maximum: A region of higher relative wind flow within a *jet stream.* Jet maximums are sometimes associated with *short waves.*

jet streak: A streak of *cirrus* clouds, visible on satellite imagery, associated with a *jet max.*

jet stream: Currents of fast-moving air located at various heights in the atmosphere. Including the polar, subtropical, mid-level, low-level and nocturnal jets. Some features associated with jet streams enhance storm development by pulling air upward (*divergence*) and help to move *precipitation* downwind and away from the *updraft,* thus venting the storm and allowing it to remain strong. Lower level jet streams can assist in creating *directional* and *speed shear* and in importing moisture.

knuckles: [slang] Lumpy, knuckle-like cloud protrusions on the edge of an *anvil* cloud or on the underside portion of *backsheared anvil.* These cloud features indicate a rapid expansion of the anvil due to the presence of a strong *updraft.*

landspout: [slang] A small, usually weak *tornado* that does not generally arise from an organized *storm-scale* rotation or a visible *wall cloud.*

Lazbuddie event: [slang-Faidley] A multiple-tornado event which occurs near Lazbuddie, Texas, a small west Texas town that was the scene of two rare multiple-tornado and *carousel events* in May of 1991 and June of 1995.

Lazbuddie maneuver: [slang-Faidley] The technique of following developing storms along the *dryline* (in west Texas) as they move east, but staying in position to observe, and possibly intercept, more violent storms that may form to the west. Named after Lazbuddie, Texas. [See *Lazbuddie event.*]

leader (stepped): See *lightning.*

leaning tower: A vertically oriented *cumulus* or *cumulonimbus tower* that leans downwind as it develops. This may imply favorable *wind shear.*

left mover: A storm which moves to the left of the dominant steering winds. Compare to *right mover.*

LEWP: See *Line Echo Wave Pattern.*

lid: Same as *cap.*

life cycle: 1. A thunderstorm's life cycle, consisting of *towering cumulus* stage *(updrafting),* mature stage and dissipating stage (predominate *outflow* or *downdrafting.*) 2. The life cycle of a tornado.
3. The life cycle of any other type of storm.

lifted index (LI): A commonly used measurement of atmospheric *instability,* where negative numbers represent a higher probability of severe weather. LIs less than -5 are generally associated with a higher probability of severe weather. (Technical note: The LI is the difference in temperature between the 500 mb temperature and that of a rising *air parcel.*)

lifting: 1. Parcel: The upward forcing of a small *parcel* of air, caused by local effects (e.g., topography, *outflow boundaries,* etc.) and/or local heating. 2. Large scale: The upward forcing associated with *dynamics* such as lifting on the east side of *troughs.*

lifting mechanism(s): Any number of *storm, meso-* or *synoptic-scale* mechanisms, processes or phenomena which may cause or assist in *lifting,* e.g., *dynamics* and *localized forcing.*

lightning (LGT): An abrupt, bright flash of light generated by the flow of electrons between oppositely charged regions of a *cumulonimbus* cloud, or between the cloud and the ground, etc.

Types of lightning and miscellaneous terminology:

lgt. **ball:** An unusual form of lightning that appears as a "ball" or luminous sphere about the size of a grapefruit. It typically has a lifetime of a few seconds. The physics of ball lightning are unknown.

lgt. **bead:** Also called "chain" lightning. A phenomenon in which the lightning channel appears to break up or fragment into separate sections. The nature of bead lightning is a mystery. (Author's note: I have witnessed and filmed bead lightning on a number of occasions. It is my observation that bead lightning is the luminous afterglow of the breakdown of the main channels.)

lgt. **blue jet:** Flashes that appear over thunderstorms in narrow beams, fans, sprays or sometimes as cones of light, which give off a purple or blue hue. Some of these flashes have been reported to travel upward, from the top of the storm to an altitude of around 20 miles. (Note: Although blue jets are associated with thunderstorms, their exact classification is still debatable.) [Associated with *red sprites.*]

lgt. **bolt:** A lightning strike or *flash.*

lgt. **"bolt from the blue":** 1. An unexpected lightning strike occurring several miles from the main thunderstorm in a rainfree area. 2. Phenomenon. A lightning flash originating from clear blue skies, without a visible storm.

lgt. **branched:** A lightning discharge with multiple branches extending outward from the main bolt, often in a root-like fashion. [Compare to *non-branched.*]

lgt. **bulber:** [slang-Faidley] A large, isolated thunderhead that lights up like a light bulb. This type of lightning is also called "sheet" lightning.

lgt. **CA:** Cloud-to-air, or "air discharge." A lightning discharge from a cloud that does not touch the ground and has no *return stroke.*

lgt. **CC:** Cloud-in-cloud, or cloud-to-cloud. A lightning discharge between the positive and negative regions of a cloud. Also called "intracloud."

lgt. **CG:** Cloud-to-ground. A lightning discharge between the earth and a cloud. Consisting of *positive* and *negative charges.*

lgt. **CS:** Cloud-to-structure. [slang-Faidley] A lightning strike to a structure or building.

lgt. **chain:** See *bead* lightning.

lgt. **channel:** The path of electrical discharge between the cloud and the ground, etc. The channel is generally an inch or less in diameter.

lgt. **continuous:** Lightning which flashes *CC*, *CG* or *CA* in a continuous manner. Continuous lightning is usually indicative of severe storms.

lgt. **crawling-crawlers:** [slang-Rhoden] Lightning that "crawls" under and next to the storm's *anvil* or the base of a storm. (Anvil crawlers.) Also called "spider" lightning [slang-Faidley].

lgt. **dart leader:** See *stepped leader.*

lgt. **flash:** The total visible part of lightning, consisting of one or more *strokes.*

lgt. **forked:** [slang] Same as *multiple branch.*

lgt. **green flash:** A lightning strike to an electrical transformer which causes a momentary greenish glow in the sky. (The color is thought to be caused by the vaporization of copper.) [Note: The term green flash also applies to a rare optical phenomenon at sunset.]

lgt. **heat:** The illumination of distant storm clouds (or the sky) by lightning, that is so far from the observer that no distinct lightning *channel* can be seen and no *thunder* heard.

lgt. **lightning rod:** A metal rod or series of rods placed on top of structures to route lightning energy harmlessly into the ground.

lgt. **mega-bolt:** [slang-Faidley] A powerful and/or nearby lightning strike.

lgt. **multiple ground point:** A lightning *flash* that branches out to have several strike points on the ground (as opposed to a single strike point). Also called "multiple channel," "branched" and "forked" lightning.

lgt. **multiple stroke:** A lightning *flash* consisting of two or more separate *strokes.* As opposed to a single stroke, multiple strokes often appear to flicker. Also called "machine gun" lightning [slang-Faidley].

lgt. **negative CG:** A lightning *stroke* which carries a negative charge between the cloud and the ground. The most common of the *negative/positive* charges.

lgt. **non-branched:** A lightning discharge consisting of a branchless *channel.* [Compare to *branched.*]

lgt. **NSG lightning:** Non-storm generated lightning. [slang-Faidley] Lightning not associated with thunderstorms, e.g., volcanic eruptions, nuclear explosions, dust storms, snow storms and smoke plumes from large fires.

lgt. **positive CG:** A lightning stroke which carries a positive charge between the cloud and the ground, as opposed to the more common *negative* charge. Positive CGs may occur more frequently in some severe thunderstorms.

lgt. **red sprites:** Associated with *Blue jets.* Red sprites are blood-red flashes that appear above the tops of thunderstorms. They sometimes have blue tendrils dangling from the bottom. Red sprites have been reported to extend upward to about 60 miles. (Note: Although red sprites are associated with thunderstorms, their exact classification is still debatable.) [Associated with *blue jets.*]

lgt. **return stroke:** The intensely luminous lightning streamer which propagates upward from the ground to the cloud, following the pathway of the *stepped leader* or *dart leader.* (What we see as lightning.) A lightning *flash* is composed of one or more individual strokes, or discharges, between the cloud and ground, etc. The return stroke travels from the ground to the cloud in about 1/10,000 second. Also called "ground flash."

lgt. **ribbon:** When a *CG* flash is moved sideways by high winds, between individual *strokes.* This horizontal movement of strokes often creates a series of identical, separated *strikes.*

lgt. **sheet:** Lightning which illuminates the interior of a thunderstorm's clouds, giving the appearance of "sheets" of lightning. Also called "bulber" [slang-Faidley].

lgt. **single stroke:** A single lightning *stroke.* As opposed to a *multiple stroke.*

lgt. **spider:** See *crawling.*

lgt. **stepped leader:** Also called "dart leader." A low-luminosity, downward-moving spark which travels from the cloud to the ground in rapid steps. The leader is made visible as a lightning flash, or *return stroke*(s), as it touches the ground and a flow of electrons moves along the established lightning *channel.* Note: In rare instances, the leader travels from the ground to the cloud, as an upward-initiated stroke.

lgt. **staccato:** [slang] A powerful, single *flash CG* lightning strike of short duration.

lgt. **strike:** A lightning *flash,* or the strike point of a lightning flash.

lgt. **stroke:** See *return stroke.*

lgt. **upward-initiated:** This type of lightning branches upward as opposed to the downward branching of the usual cloud-to-ground strike. This form of lightning usually initiates from metal towers, mountain peaks and tall buildings. [Also see *stepped leader.*]

lightning rod: See *lightning.*

LLJ: See *Low-level jet stream.*

line echo wave pattern (LEWP): A radar term used to describe a bulge in a line of thunderstorm cells, appearing as a wave-shaped kink, usually associated with *squall lines.* Strong and damaging winds may be associated with an LEWP.

loaded gun: [slang] A term used to describe an extremely unstable atmosphere that is contained by a strong *cap,* which is not likely to be broken. But if the cap is broken, there is the distinct possibility of isolated, violent storms.

long wave (trough): A south-to-north *trough* in the normal west-to-east flow aloft which is characterized by a large wavelength (generally 2,500 to 5,000 miles) and, usually, long duration. *Short waves* are sometimes embedded in the long wave flow.

lowering: Any lowering under a thunderstorm's base, but specifically a *wall cloud.*

low-level jet/stream (LLJ): *Jet streams* located in the lower third of the *troposphere.* Such jets can often assist in creating favorable *directional* and *speed shear* and the importation of moisture.

low-precipitation supercell (LP): A type of *supercell* storm. Characterized by low levels of visible *precipitation.* LPs are often breathtaking storms because of their corkscrewed, *striated* cloud structures and highly visible, low-level *updraft* features. The tornadoes that LPs produce are generally not as strong as the tornadoes generated by *HP* and *classic supercells.*

low pressure area/systems: A pool of air that rotates cyclonically around a center of lower *barometric pressure,* occurring in *mesoscale* to *synoptic-scales.* Clouds and storms are often associated with the rising air of low pressure areas. Seen on weather maps as "L." Systems are often referred to as: *surface low, upper-level low, cutoff low, mesolow.* [Compare with *high pressure.*]

LP supercell: See *Low-precipitation supercell.*

main storm/tower/updraft: The most significant or dominant storm, *cumulonimbus tower* or *updraft* within a specific group.

mammatus clouds: Rounded, sac-like protrusions hanging from the underside of a cloud. They are often seen under an *anvil* cloud. These clouds do not produce severe weather but can indicate turbulent winds aloft.

mature stage: The middle of three stages in the *life cycle* of a thunderstorm, when the *updrafts* and *downdrafts* are co-existing. Term is also used to describe the mature stage of a tornado's life cycle.

maxi (tornado): A large, damaging tornado.

MCC: See *Mesoscale convective complex.*

MCS: See *Mesoscale convective system.*

media chaser(s): Journalists or news crews who occasionally chase storms as part of their normal news/weather gathering operations. [Also see *hobbyist, professional, outlaw, scientific chasers* and *spotters.]*

mega-bolt: See *lightning.*

merger: When single storms (or cells) merge, creating a stronger storm.

mesocyclone: A radar term (used extensively by chasers and spotters) for a *storm-scale* region of rotation, typically 2-6 miles in diameter and often found on the southwestern part of a *supercell.* The new *Doppler* radar can detect mesocyclones that can extend far upward into the storm, allowing forecasters to issue *tornado warnings* based on predetermined thresholds.

mesohigh: A region of cold outflow air with high relative air pressures generally found in the wake of a thunderstorm. Mesohighs can inhibit further storm development.

mesolow: A small surface *low pressure system* generally less than 100 miles in diameter. Mesolows may enhance storm potential by increasing *moisture convergence* and providing low-level wind *veering.*

mesonet: A vast network of manned and unmanned weather stations that provide extensive surface weather data.

mesoscale: A scale of size referring to weather systems that are generally from 100 to 1000 square miles in size. Mesoscale systems are smaller than *synoptic-scale* systems but larger than *storm-scale* systems.

mesoscale convective complex (MCC): A large complex of thunderstorms which meets certain criteria, including persistence for over six hours. MCCs usually reach their peak intensity at night. During the southwestern U.S. *monsoon,* MCCs will occasionally form over Mexico and move into Arizona and New Mexico during the evening hours, bringing flooding rains, damaging winds and intense lightning.

mesoscale convective system (MCS): A complex or cluster of thunderstorms generally smaller than an *MCC,* which does not meet MCC criteria.

microburst: A small, concentrated *downburst* from a thunderstorm, that affects an area of usually less than 2.5 miles across. Most microbursts last less than five minutes, but they can produce winds of over 100 mph. Microbursts can cause extreme *wind shear,* posing a substantial hazard to aircraft. From 1964 to 1993, at least 30 major airline accidents have been caused by microbursts. Sometimes, the winds from a microburst will create a fast-moving cloud of dust known as a *dust foot.* [Also see *wet and dry microbursts.*]

millibar (mb): A unit of *air pressure.*

missile: Any object picked up and carried by high winds.

models: A computer-generated weather forecast, which covers daily and long-range predictions. The NGM, AVN, ETA and the MRF are common types.

moderate risk (of severe weather): A forecast issued by the *Severe Local Storms Unit* (SELS) in the *convective outlook.* A moderate risk is noted when severe weather is expected to affect between five and ten percent of an outlined area. [Also see *slight risk* and *high risk.*]

moist axis: See *triple point.*

moist tongue: [slang] A tongue-shaped area of moist air which protrudes into a drier region.

moisture: The water vapor content of the air, most commonly measured as the *dew point* and *relative humidity.*

moisture convergence: A measure of the degree to which moist air is converging into an area. Localized areas of moisture convergence can favor thunderstorm development and are often targeted by chasers if other necessary weather *elements* are present.

monsoon: A persistent seasonal wind shift, e.g., the southwestern U.S. monsoon, where the clockwise circulation around the Subtropical High brings moisture from Northern Mexico into the desert southwest.

multicell storms: A thunderstorm consisting of two or more *cells,* usually occurring in a low *wind shear* environment. The majority of thunderstorms are multi-cellular.

multi-line storm: Same as *squall line.*

multiple-vortex tornado: A tornado in which two or more vortices are present at the same time. Multiple-vortex tornadoes can be especially damaging.

mushroom: [slang] An *anvil* or *cumulonimbus tower* top, especially those that begin to roll over slightly.

National Hurricane Center (NHC): An *NOAA* organization responsible for the issuance of tropical weather analyses, watches and warnings. The NHC was relocated from Coral Gables, Florida to Miami, Florida in 1995, and renamed the *Tropical Prediction Center* (TPC).

National Oceanic and Atmospheric Administration (NOAA): A Department of Commerce administration that oversees the *NWS*, *NHC* and other weather-related agencies.

National Severe Storms Forecast Center (NSSFC): A government agency located in Kansas City, Missouri. The NSSFC issues tornado and severe thunderstorm watches, and the *SELS convective outlooks* for the U.S. Note: The NSSFC is to be split into two divisions in the late 1990s: The *Storm Prediction Center* (SPC) and the *Aviation Weather Center* (AWC.) The SPC will eventually delegate the issuance of severe weather *watches* to local *WSFOs*. The SPC will, however, continue to issue convective outlooks.

National Severe Storms Laboratory (NSSL): Located in Norman, Oklahoma. A government-sponsored research center for severe weather.

National Weather Service (NWS): An organization of *NOAA* that is responsible for issuing information, advisories, local forecasts and warnings to the public.

National Weather Service Forecast Office (NWSFO): An *NWS* office responsible for issuing forecasts.

negative-tilt trough: A *trough* in the upper atmosphere with a base east of its axis (as opposed to a *positive-tilt trough).* This configuration causes substantial *lifting* on the east side of the trough. Many significant severe weather outbreaks are associated with negative-tilt troughs.

net: Short for network. See *spotter net.*

NEXRAD: See *NEXt-Generation Weather RADar.*

next generation weather radar: (NEXRAD) An advanced weather radar network installed throughout the country that utilizes *Doppler Radar.*

NHC: See *National Hurricane Center.*

NOAA: See *National Oceanic and Atmospheric Administration.*

NSSFC: See *National Severe Storms Forecast Center.*

NSSL: See *National Severe Storms Laboratory.*

NWS: See *National Weather Service.*

omega block: A stalled, *synoptic-scale ridge*, shaped like the Greek letter omega. Depending on its positioning, an omega block can have varied effects on severe weather.

open eye wall: A hurricane *eye wall* with one or more gaps or deformities, denoting a weakness in its structure (as opposed to a *closed eye wall).*

open trough/wave: A U-shaped *trough* without closed *isobars.* Open troughs are a common source of lifting during the *chase season.* [Compare with *closed low.*]

orographic lifting (storms): When mountains, hills or other high terrain act as a barrier to the wind flow, causing the air to ascend. Storms may result from such lifting if other necessary *elements* are present.

orphan anvil: [slang] An *anvil* from a dissipating thunderstorm, without a storm body below it.

outbreak: A severe weather event where numerous tornadoes are produced. The Super Outbreak of April 3 and 4, 1974 spawned over 148 tornadoes which swept across 11 states, killing 315 people.

outflow: Rain-cooled air (and moisture) from a thunderstorm.

outflow boundaries: The leading edge of rain-cooled air and moisture spreading out from a thunderstorm. Outflow boundaries may serve as an important *lifting* mechanism. Thus, they may serve as a focus for new storm development.

outflow dominant storm: A dead or dying storm where *outflow* air prevails.

outlaw (chasers): [slang] Often reckless chasers who chase only for the thrill. They generally have no interest in meteorology or *spotting.* [Also see *media, hobbyist, professional, scientific chasers* and *spotters.]*

out-of-phase: When one or more *elements* required for the production of severe weather is absent or mistimed. [Also see *timing.*]

overshooting top: A dome-shaped cloud that appears above the *anvil* cloud, over the region of the most intense *updraft.* The collapse of an overshooting top is sometimes associated with *tornadogenesis.* Also called "penetrating top."

panhandle surprise: [slang-Feely] A severe storm(s) that develops in the Texas panhandle with little or no warning, especially on days when severe weather is not expected. [Similar to *six o'clock magic* and *West Texas magic.]*

parcel: See *air parcel.*

PDS: Particularly dangerous situation. A phrase, or enhanced wording, used in the *convective outlook* text. PDS generally refers to *high risk* days, when the expected storms are likely to be of a very threatening nature.

pea soup: [slang] Chaser's terminology for visibility obscuring drizzle or light *precipitation*, generally associated with decaying storms. Also called "grunge."

pedestal cloud: [slang] Same as *wall cloud.*

penetrating top: Same as *overshooting top.*

pileus: A flat, concave-shaped cloud sometimes seen above a convective *tower.*

plates: Similar to *striations.* Laminar cloud layers sometimes seen near the base of storms, resembling stacks of plates.

plume: [slang] A thunderstorm *anvil.* Term is occasionally used to describe areas of *capping* warm air or *moist tongues.*

pops: [slang] Probability of *precipitation.*

positive-tilt trough: A *trough* in the upper atmosphere with a base west of its axis (as opposed to a *negative-tilt trough).* Positive-tilt troughs may have less *divergence* on the eastern side than negative-tilt troughs.

precipitation: Any form of water particles that falls from the atmosphere, including rain, hail, snow, drizzle, etc.

professional chaser: An experienced storm chaser, who forecasts and chases all forms of severe weather, as a full-time occupation, and whose main income is derived from storm chasing. [Also see *media, hobbyist, outlaw, scientific chasers* and *spotters.]*

profiler: A relatively compact (usually 40 by 40 feet) array of radar antennas which beam radio waves upward at different angles, measuring slight changes in air density. Profilers are capable of measuring wind direction and speeds at 72 different levels up to around 10 miles, every 5 minutes, even in clear skies.

Public Information Statement (PUI): A statement issued by the Weather Service pertaining to dangerous weather conditions. Such statements are sometimes issued on *high risk* days.

pulse storm: A thunderstorm that goes through a single *life cycle* and dissipates. Usually lasting less than one hour. As opposed to a *cyclic* thunderstorm.

punch out bag: [slang-Faidley] A small water resistant bag attached to a chaser, which holds valuable exposed film and/or a wallet. Designed as a final resort, save-all if a chaser must flee a vehicle to seek shelter.

RACES: Radio Amateur Civil Emergency Service. A group of amateur radio operators who assist in relaying severe weather information. [Also see *storm spotter* and *spotter net.*]

radiosonde: An electronic sensing instrument, about the size of a shoe box, which is attached to a large helium-filled balloon and is released twice a day by selected *NWS* offices. As the devices ascend, they send temperature, pressure and humidity data back to a receiving unit on the ground. Wind directions and speeds are also measured by tracking the position of the balloon. The data is critical in making weather maps and measuring *instability.* [Also see *soundings.*]

rain curtains: Shafts or walls of heavy precipitation.

rain foot: A horizontal bulging near the surface in a *precipitation* shaft, which forms a foot-shaped prominence. A rain foot is a visual indication of a *wet microburst.*

rainfree base: The *updraft* area of a storm, generally located on the southwestern flank of a northeast moving storm, appearing as a horizontal, dark base which has no visible *precipitation* beneath it. *Tornadogenesis* often begins in this region in the form of a *wall cloud.*

rain shaft: A thick *rain curtain.*

rear-flank downdraft (RFD): A region of dry air subsiding on the back side of, and wrapping around, a *mesocyclone.* It is often seen as a *clear slot* wrapping around the *wall cloud.* The development of an RFD is considered fundamental in the formation of a tornado.

recreational chasers: Same as *hobbyist chaser(s).*

red box: [slang] A tornado *watch* box. Also called "red watch."

red sprites: See *lightning.*

return flow: The return of moist, Gulf of Mexico air into the Plains.

return stroke: See *lightning.*

ribbon (lightning): See *lightning.*

ridge: An elongated area of atmospheric *high pressure.* Strong "ridging," and the stable, sinking air associated with it, is usually associated with fair weather.

ridged out: [slang] Same as *death ridge.*

right mover: A thunderstorm that moves appreciably to the right, relative to the main steering winds and to other nearby storms. Right movers are sometimes associated with a higher potential for severe weather. *Supercells* are often right movers.

ring of fire: The edges of a large *high pressure ridge* where thunderstorms develop, especially in late summer.

ripple: [slang] A small *disturbance* which is difficult to detect or predict. Such disturbances can trigger unexpected severe weather events.

ripple effect: The theory that seemingly small events can set off a chain reaction of natural events which ultimately have some major effect on nature, i.e., weather. For example, a butterfly flapping its wings in Canada may eventually cause a tornado in Texas. Chasers generally do not apply the ripple effect theory to their forecasts.

roar: The sound created by a tornado or hurricane.

roll cloud: A low, horizontal tube-shaped cloud usually associated with a *gust front.*

rope funnel: A narrow, often contorted condensation funnel usually associated with the decaying stage of a tornado.

roping out: [slang] A term used to describe the final stages of a tornado's *life cycle* where the funnel takes on a rope-like shape.

Saffir-Simpson Hurricane Damage Potential Scale: A scale developed in the early 1970s by Herbert Saffir, an engineer, and Robert Simpson, former director of the *NHC,* to measure hurricane intensity.

Category 1 : Minimal damage. Barometric pressure: 28.94+ inches, sustained winds of 74-95 mph, storm surge of 4-5 feet.

Category 2 : Moderate damage. Barometric pressure: 28.50-28.91 inches, sustained winds of 96-110 mph, storm surge of 6-8 feet.

Category 3: Extensive damage. Barometric pressure: 27.91-28.47 inches, sustained winds of 111-130 mph, storm surge of 9-12 feet.

Category 4: Extreme damage. Barometric pressure: 27.17-27.88 inches, sustained winds of 131-155, storm surge of 13-18 feet.

Category 5: Catastrophic damage. Barometric pressure: <27.17 inches, sustained winds of >155 mph, storm surge of >18 feet.

sand blast: 1. Main. Windblown beach sand caused by a tropical storm or hurricane. 2. Windblown sand or grit caused by thunderstorm winds.

satellite (tornado/funnel): 1. [slang] A secondary (or more) tornado or funnel cloud that forms from the same storm while a main tornado is still on the ground. Satellites are usually associated with *HP* and *cyclic supercells,* which may have several areas of rotation. 2. A weather satellite, such as the *geostationary orbiting earth satellite.* [Also see *carrousel event.*]

scanner: A radio receiver that scans a large bank of preset frequencies. Chasers utilize scanners to monitor *NWS* weather reports, storm spotter transmissions and emergency information.

scientific chaser: A person who occasionally chases storms for research. [Also see *media, professional, outlaw, hobbyist chasers* and *spotters.]*

scud clouds: See *fractus* clouds.

SELS: See *SEvere Local Storms Unit.*

Severe Local Storms Unit (SELS): A group of meteorologists with the National Severe Storms Forecast Center (*NSSFC*) in Kansas City, Missouri. SELS is responsible for issuing *convective outlooks* and discussions several times daily and is responsible for issuing all *tornado* and *severe thunderstorm watches* for the U.S. Note: SELS is scheduled to be dismantled in the mid 90s. Regional *WSFOs* will then have the responsibility of issuing watches. The *SPC* will issue *convective outlooks* and provide WSFOs with watch issuance guidance.

severe thunderstorm: A thunderstorm that produces one or more of the following: tornadoes, hail three-quarters of an inch or more in diameter, or winds of at least 58 mph. Structural wind damage reports or radar indications may also imply the occurrence of a severe thunderstorm. Of the 100,000 thunderstorms which form over the U.S. each year, only 10% reach severe criteria.

severe weather outlooks: Detailed discussions issued by the *NWS,* outlining the possibilities of severe weather for a specific region.

Shadow Chaser ™: The nickname for storm chaser Warren Faidley's customized chase vehicle.

shear: Same as *wind shear.*

shear funnel: See *funnel cloud.*

sheet (lightning): See *lightning.*

shelf cloud: A low horizontal cloud associated with the *gust front.*

short wave (trough): A horizontal migratory mid- and upper-*tropospheric disturbance* with a wavelength on the order of 500 to 1,000 miles. Upper-tropospheric *divergence* and mid-tropospheric upward motion are often found on the forward (eastern) side of short waves. Short waves can trigger severe weather if other necessary *elements* are present. [Also see *long wave.*]

signature: The term used to describe the various reflectivity patterns seen on a radar screen. *Hook echoes* and *bow echoes* are examples.

six o'clock magic: [slang] The almost mystical formation of storms and tornadoes just when the chase day seems to be a *bust.* [Similar to *West Texas magic* and *panhandle surprise.*]

Skywarn: The official name for the *spotter* groups who report severe weather information directly to the *NWS* or *spotter coordinator.*

slight risk (of severe weather): A forecast issued by the *Severe Local Storms Unit* (SELS) in the *convective outlook.* A slight risk is noted when severe weather is expected to affect between two and five percent of an outlined area. [Also see *moderate risk* and *high risk.*]

sloshing dryline: A *dryline* that moves from east to west, then back again for several days, causing repeated severe weather.

sorcering: [slang-Runyon] The over-forecasting and wishful-thinking that chasers sometimes execute during their forecasts.

sounding: A plot of the vertical profile of temperature, pressures, *dew points* and winds above a fixed location. Soundings are used extensively in severe weather forecasting and are important in measuring *instability, wind shear* and the strength of the *cap.* Soundings are made from data gathered from devices called *radiosondes.*

souvenirs: [slang] Damage (battle scars) to a chaser's vehicle, such as hail dents.

speed shear: The component of *wind shear* which is due to an increase in wind speed with height (from the ground upward). Favorable speed shear in combination with *directional shear* in the low levels of the *troposphere* is important in the development of *mesocyclones* and in augmenting *updraft* strength. [Also see *helicity.*]

spiral bands: Bands of thunderstorms that spiral around the center of a *hurricane.* They are seen on satellite images as the arms that spiral inward toward the center and are typically 3 to 30 miles wide and 50 to 300 miles long. Term may also apply to such bands associated with land mass thunderstorms.

splitting storm: A thunderstorm that splits into two storms, which follow diverging paths (a *left* and a *right mover).*

spotter: Same as *storm spotter.*

spotter coordinator(s): A person or group who takes reports from storm spotters in the field and relays the information to the *NWS* or the local emergency management agency.

spotter net. (network): The *ham radio* communications network used by *spotters.* Also called RACES (Radio Amateur Civil Emergency Service), ARES (Amateur Radio Emergency Service), and *Skywarn.*

squall line: A solid or nearly solid line or band of thunderstorms that can stretch for hundreds of miles. They typically occur 50 to 100 miles in advance of strong *cold fronts* in the spring. Although the thunderstorms that comprise squall lines can produce all forms of severe weather, they are generally poor tornado producers and are often avoided by chasers. The thunderstorms (or *supercells*) that form in front of a squall line can sometimes be especially dangerous.

stabilized atmosphere: When atmospheric conditions do not favor the *lifting* of *air parcels.* For example, a strong *ridge* is present. Opposite of *destabilized.*

stepped leader: See *lightning.*

staccato (lightning): See *lightning.*

stacked low: A *cut off, low pressure system* where the *upper-level low* is centered over or near the main *surface low.* Such lows are generally not associated with substantial severe weather due to the lack of directional *shear.*

stair-stepped: [slang] Any cloud feature with an incremental increase, or stair-stepping appearance, such as the *flanking line.*

steamnado: [slang] A weak, non-storm-generated vortex associated with rising steam or fog, often associated with winter weather features.

stock photography agency: A company that markets the reproduction rights to photographs from a library of existing images.

storm chaser: A person who chases storms. [Also see *media, professional, outlaw, hobbyist, scientific chasers* and *spotters.*]

storm-scale: A scale referring to weather systems with sizes on the order of individual thunderstorms (1-100 square miles).

storm spotter: Trained volunteers or qualified observers, including *ham radio* operators, chasers, law enforcement and fire department personnel, who chase and/or observe storms near their communities or jurisdiction and relay information to a volunteer coordinator or directly to the *NWS.* [Also see *spotter net., media, professional, outlaw, hobbyist* and *scientific chasers.]*

storm surge: Rapidly rising ocean levels associated with *tropical storms* and *hurricanes.* Storm surges are generally a hurricane's most deadly offspring.

***Stormtrack*:** A bi-monthly, homemade publication about storm chasing. Founded in 1977 by Dave Hoadley, a pioneer storm chaser.

stovepipe: [slang] An elongated tornado that takes on the shape of a stovepipe.

straight-line winds: Generally, any wind not associated with rotation. [Compare with *microburst* and *downdraft.*]

stratocumulus: Low-level clouds appearing as stratiform with lumpy, rounded masses or in patches with blue sky between them. Stratocumulus often imply the presence of a thick *moisture* layer near the ground.

striations (cloud): Laminar grooves or channels in cloud formations, often occurring in helical bands. Striations can reveal the presence of rotation. Striations may be seen with *barber pole* or *corkscrew* effects. [Also see *LP* storms.]

suction spot: A small but intense *vortex* within a tornadic circulation. Term is sometimes used by chasers to denote the dust or *debris cloud* below a *funnel cloud.*

sundog: A form of parhelia. A pale, colored spot sometimes seen to the right and/or the left of the sun, usually occurring at sunset and sunrise when a thin layer of clouds are present. They are caused by the refraction of light passing through ice crystals. At night they are called "moon dogs."

supercell storm: A relatively long-lived thunderstorm with a persistent rotating *updraft.* Consisting of *high-precipitation* (HP), *low-precipitation* (LP), *classic* and hybrids. Supercells are the most uncommon of thunderstorm types but are responsible for a high percentage of violent tornadoes, large *hail* and damaging *straight-line winds.* Many supercells do not fit into a specific category but are hybrids. Some supercells transform from one type to another. Supercells may become *cyclic,* producing multiple tornadoes.

surface heating: The heating of the ground and the reflection of heat caused by solar radiation. Surface heating adds to *instability* by assisting in localized *lifting.*

surface low: A *low pressure system* near the earth's surface.

surface plot: A simple weather map that has surface data for fixed locations. The data usually includes: *dew points,* surface winds, pressures, cloud cover, weather conditions and temperatures. Storm chasers use surface plots, which are updated each hour, to note <u>changes</u> in surface conditions.

SVR: Severe.

swirl marks: The circular marks left in an open field or *debris zone* following a tornado.

synoptic-scale: A size scale referring to weather systems with horizontal dimensions of generally 500 miles or greater. The majority of *high pressure* and *low pressure* systems are examples. [Also see *mesoscale* and *storm-scale.*]

tail cloud: A tail-shaped cloud that sometimes forms on the north or northeast side of a *wall cloud.*

tail-end Charlie: [slang] The thunderstorm at the southernmost end of a *squall line* or other line of thunderstorms. These storms have a better chance of producing severe weather, because the southerly flow of wind and moisture feeding into them is unimpeded.

tails: Small, needle-like *funnel clouds.*

thermal axis: See *triple point.*

thermodynamics: The three-dimensional thermal and moisture structure of the atmosphere that determines whether the atmosphere is *stable* or *unstable.* Thermodynamics are often visualized by means of a graphical plot of the *sounding.*

The Weather Channel: A cable network providing television's only 24-hour indepth weather coverage. The Weather Channel also provides weather related home video products, interactive telephone services, on-line and multimedia products.

threat area: A region where severe weather is possible.

thunder: The sound made by the lightning channel as it superheats the surrounding air, causing it to violently expand, thus creating pressure variations that produce an audible sound.

thunderhead: A *cumulonimbus* cloud.

thundersnow: A snowstorm accompanied by thunder.

timing: The ultimate deciding factor in the production of severe weather. All of the *elements* must come together at the precise moment in order for chaseable storms to occur. Also see *out-of-phase.*

tornadic vortex signature (TVS): A *Doppler* radar *signature* that indicates intense, concentrated rotation within a storm. Specific criteria involving strength, vertical depth and time continuity must be met in order for a signature to become a TVS. A TVS implies the possibility of a tornado, but it cannot confirm that a tornado is on the ground.

tornado (TOR): A violently rotating column of air <u>in contact with the ground</u>. Note: A condensation *funnel* does not need to be in contact with the ground to constitute a tornado. A *dust whirl* or a rotating *debris cloud* underneath a thunderstorm generally confirms a tornado, even in the absence of a condensation funnel. However, in certain circumstances the *NWS* may issue a tornado warning if a tornadic signature is detected by radar (rotation lowering through the storm toward the ground) or if spotters report a rapidly rotating *wall cloud* or a *funnel cloud* moving toward a populated area.

tornado alley: An area of the southern, northern Great Plains and east central United States where the highest level of tornadic activity occurs. [Also see *hot zone.*]

tornado family: A group of tornadoes associated with a single storm or storm event.

tornadogenesis: The formation of a *tornado.*

tornado, names: Unlike hurricanes, tornadoes are not given official names. They are generally remembered (named) from the towns that they hit (or occurred near), the type of event or the geographical areas where they happened. For example, the horrific killer tornado that destroyed Xenia, Ohio, in April of 1974, will forever be remembered as the "Xenia" tornado. The overall outbreak that spawned the Xenia tornado and 147 additional tornadoes has become known as the "Super Outbreak."

tornado outbreak: When multiple tornadoes are produced by the same *synoptic-scale* storm system, generally on the same day.

tornado/funnel shape and slang names: Bowl, cigar, cone, cylinder, elephant trunk, hourglass, *landspout,* loop, *multiple vortex,* needle, *Oz,* rope, segmented, sheathed, stovepipe, drill press, tail, tube, V-shaped, *waterspout,* wedge, wire.

tornado siren: A loud siren, usually producing a high-low, air-raid type sound, which is activated by local governments when a tornado is seen approaching a populated area. Some cities activate the siren a second time, in a slightly different manner, to signal an "all clear."

tornado warning: A tornado warning means that a tornado has been reported on the ground by spotters (or is in the process of forming via radar criteria.) A tornado warning indicates that an immediate danger exists, and people should take quick action to save lives. [Compare with *tornado watch.*]

tornado watch: A tornado watch identifies a relatively large geographical area in which tornadoes are possible. Tornado watches generally cover an area approximately 140 miles wide by 200 miles long. [Compare with *tornado warning.*]

TOTO: TOtable Tornado Observatory. A 400-lb. package of weather instruments encased in a protective drum, designed to be placed by scientists in the path of a tornado. TOTO was deployed from 1981 through 1983 by *NSSL* chase teams in an effort to collect data from the interior of a twister. Although it was sideswiped by a tornado, it never took a direct hit.

tower: A vertically developing *cumulus* or *cumulonimbus* cloud. Well-structured towers are the predecessors to thunderstorms and are the initial convective development that chasers watch for. [Also see *turkey towers* and *leaning towers.*]

towering cumulus (TCU): A vertically developing *cumulus* cloud without an anvil. Also called *tower.*

towering cumulus stage: The first of the three stages of a thunderstorm's *life cycle.*

TPC: See *Tropical Prediction Center.*

train echo/train echo line pattern: A radar term used to describe a line or cluster of storms (or reforming storms) that move over the same area. Such patterns may cause flooding.

transformer (storm): [slang-Faidley] A weak storm that undergoes a sudden transformation into a stronger storm, e.g., *multicell* into a *supercell.* This change is often caused by increasing *dynamics* as the afternoon progresses, or the storm moves into a more *unstable* environment, e.g., favorable *wind shear* or higher *dew points.*

triggering mechanism/trigger: Any number of *storm, meso* or *synoptic-scale* mechanisms that initiate thunderstorm development by enhancing the vertical velocity or *lift* in the atmosphere. Examples include: approaching *short waves, low pressure* areas, localized *lifting,* and *cold pools.* [Related to *focusing mechanisms* and *forcing.*]

triple point: The intersection of the center line of warmest surface temperatures (thermal axis), the ridge of highest *dew points* (moist axis) and a *boundary.* This area is sometimes favored for severe storm development if other necessary *elements* are present.

tropical cyclone: A *hurricane, tropical storm, typhoon* or any closed surface circulation in the tropics associated with a *low pressure system,* in which the central core is warmer than the surrounding atmosphere. [Compare to *extratropical cyclone.*]

tropical depression: A *tropical cyclone* with maximum sustained winds near the surface of less than 39 mph.

Tropical Prediction Center (TPC): Formerly the *National Hurricane Center.* An *NOAA* organization responsible for the issuance of tropical weather analyses, watches and warnings. The NHC was relocated from Coral Gables, Florida to Miami, Florida in 1995, and renamed the *Tropical Prediction Center* (TPC).

tropical storm: A *tropical cyclone* with winds from 39 to 73 mph. (At 74 mph a tropical storm officially becomes a *hurricane.*)

troposphere: The lower layer of the atmosphere, generally located from the earth's surface to around 7 miles, depending on latitude and the season. The troposphere is where most clouds and weather are located.

trough: An elongated area of *low pressure*, generally running north-south, either at the surface or aloft. [Also see *shortwave* and *long wave* troughs.]

TSTM: Thunderstorm.

turkey towers: [slang] An impressive *cumulus tower* that rapidly builds, then falls apart without becoming a storm, luring a chaser on a "wild goose chase."

turtles: Small, fortified instrument packages, shaped like a turtle's shell; designed to be placed in the path of a tornado by scientists to record meteorological data.

TVS: See *Tornadic Vortex Signature.*

typhoon: A *tropical cyclone* with winds of 74 mph or greater, located in the north Pacific, west of the International Date Line.

unstable air mass: A state in which the *thermodynamic* and moisture characteristics of an *air mass* are favorable for the creation of spontaneous upward motion and growth of a thunderstorm. The degree of stability or *instability* is determined from a consideration of plotted temperatures and *dew points* at different elevations known as a *sounding.*

updraft: The area(s) of the storm where the air is rising upward. The updraft region, or *rainfree base,* is a favorable location for the formation of *wall clouds* and *tornadoes.* The *updrafts* of some *supercells* can reach speeds of 150 mph to 175 mph.

upper-air support: [slang] Favorable *directional* and *speed shear* generally associated with the eastern portions of an upper air *trough.*

upper-level disturbance/low: See *disturbance* and *low pressure systems.*

upslope, upslope flow: An *air mass* which flows toward higher terrain; thus, it is forced to rise. If the atmosphere is *unstable*, the upslope flow may increase the thunderstorm potential. The Caprock region of west Texas and the eastern Colorado foothills are two examples of upslope terrain that often assist in *convection.*

vapor: [slang] The misty, fog-like vapor sometimes seen wrapping around a tornado, especially the *inflow* vapor tails near the ground circulation.

veer/veering (wind): An important component of *wind shear*, in which the shear consists of favorable clockwise turning (*directional shear*) of the winds aloft. Lower *tropospheric* veering is critical in the development of a storm's *mesocyclone.* [Related to *speed shear.*]

VIP: Video Integrator and Processor. A radar term, ranging from VIP-1 to VIP-6, used to describe different levels or intensities of precipitation, e.g., VIP-1 indicates light precipitation, while VIP-6 would indicate heavy rain and possible large *hail.* Note: The term VIP actually relates to the older WSR-57 and 74-C radar systems. The pre-existing VIP levels are sometimes used figuratively in conjunction with the newer *WSR-88 Doppler*, especially on television weather radar.

virga: Streaks or wisps of *precipitation* falling from a cloud.

V-shaped echo: A radar term used to describe several reflectivity *signatures* characterized by a V-shaped *echo.* V-echoes are sometimes associated with severe and supercell storms. Also called "V-notch."

vortex, vortices: 1. A rapidly-spinning column of fluid or air. 2. An area of strong rotation in the atmosphere, e.g., a *cyclone.* 3. The word vortex is also used figuratively by chasers to describe a tornado.

VORTEX: Verification of the Origins of Rotation in Tornadoes EXperiment. A large-scale research project conducted by the *NSSL* in 1994-95, to study various scientific aspects of tornadic storms.

wall cloud: A lowering from a *rainfree base.* Wall clouds can range from a fraction of a mile to nearly five miles in diameter. They are generally found on the south or southwest side of a thunderstorm, in the *updraft* or *inflow* area. Some wall clouds exhibit rapid upward and downward motion, and may ingest small nearby *fractus* clouds. Rotating wall clouds usually develop before strong or violent tornadoes and may persist from a few minutes to over an hour before producing a tornado. Wall clouds produce tornadoes less than fifty percent of the time.

warm advection: The transport of warm air into a region by horizontal winds. This increases the *instability* if the warm *advection* is occurring at the surface.

warm front: See *fronts.*

warning: Warnings are issued by the *NWS* for any type of dangerous weather, including *tornadoes, severe thunderstorms, flash floods,* river floods and high winds. A warning means that some form of hazardous weather is occurring or is imminent.

watch: Weather watches are issued by the *NWS* for *tornadoes, flash floods* and *severe thunderstorms* and winter weather. Watches are issued when weather conditions favor the development of dangerous weather. A watch should not be confused with a *warning*, which means that severe weather is already occurring.

waterspout: A *tornado* over water.

wave: 1. A *short wave*. 2. Wave on a surface *front*.

weather balloon: See *radiosonde*.

weather radio: A radio that receives the continuous broadcasts from the *NWS*, in the 162.000 MHz range. Some of these radios have a special alert feature which will activate an alarm if the weather service issues a *watch* or *warning* tone. [Also see *weather radio specific area message encoder*.]

weather radio specific area message encoder (WRSAME): A special type of *weather radio* that only broadcasts selective warnings for specific areas or counties, as defined by the user.

wedge: [slang] A tornado that takes on a wedge-shaped appearance, generally with a width that is equal to or greater than its height, as visible to the eye. Wedge-shaped tornadoes are usually of a very strong intensity.

weekend warriors: Part-time *storm chasers*. See *hobbyist chasers*.

West Texas magic: [slang] The often baffling ability of storms in west Texas to suddenly form and produce tornadoes on days when the initial meteorological indications do not support such phenomena. [Similar to *six o'clock magic* and *panhandle surprise*.]

wet microburst: As opposed to a *dry microburst*, a wet *microburst* is accompanied by heavy *precipitation* at the surface. [Also see *rain foot*.]

white harvest: [slang] A *hailstorm* which leaves a swath of *hailstones* over a field of destroyed crops.

whiteout: [slang] A *hailstorm* that causes zero visibility.

wind shear: Any sudden change in wind speed or direction. Note: The combination of favorable *speed* and *directional shear* is sometimes referred to as "favorable shear." [Also see *microburst, directional shear, speed shear* and *downdraft*.]

Wizard of Oz tornado: [slang] Any tornado that resembles the snake-like tornado from the movie *The Wizard of Oz*.

worked over: [slang] An atmosphere that has been *stabilized* by other storms, e.g., by cold *outflow*.

WRSAME: See *weather radio specific area message encoder*.

WSFO: See *National Weather Service Forecast Office*.

WSR-88D: See *Doppler radar*.

WX: Abbreviation for "weather."

x-ray: [slang-Henry] Code word for law enforcement officer. Especially those with active radar or laser guns.

Yellow brick road: Any number of highways leading to a storm, especially those which run from a southwest to northeast direction. Also roads that are flat and have few towns to slow down a chase. For example, U.S. Highway 54 which traverses the Texas and Oklahoma panhandles into Kansas.

zonal: Upper-level wind flow moving in a west-to-east direction.

Photography Credits

Tom Willett, pages 32, 84, 136, 137

Joe Towers, page 70

N.O.A.A., pages 84, 123

J.W. Smith, back cover portrait

All other photos by Warren Faidley.

ACKNOWLEDGMENTS

This book is the culmination of over four years of writing, editing, planning and research. It has been a true labor of love and the realization of an outstanding group effort.

Therefore, I would like to express my sincere gratitude to the following individuals for their assistance and encouragement, which have helped to make this book and my work possible:

José Garcia, Meteorologist In Charge, National Weather Service, Amarillo, TX

Bill Runyon, Ed Andrade and the entire staff at the National Weather Service offices in Amarillo and throughout the United States

Don Robertson, Evelyn Tyte, James Fallat, Tim and Lisa Rempe

Jeff W. Smith, Ron Pavelka, Patricia Tronstad

My chase partners: Tom Willett, Phil and Kathy Henry, Joel Ewing, John Monteverdi, Thom Trimble and all the chasers and storm spotters who have supported, educated and advised me over the years

Bill Adler and Lisa Swayne at Adler and Robin Books

Photographic Works Lab, Tucson

Louis Schwartzberg, Energy Productions, CA

John Macfie, International Stock, NY

Keith Rosenblum for his editing assistance

Wendy Stahl, Stu Ostro, Eileen Lichtenfeld and the entire staff at The Weather Channel

My family, friends, fans, teachers, agents and clients

And last, but not least, my Angels.

YOU CAN CONTACT WARREN FAIDLEY AND WEATHERSTOCK AT:

WEATHERSTOCK
PO Box 31808
Tucson, AZ 85751

or on the World Wide Web at:
http://www.indirect.com/www/storm5

CONTACT THE WEATHER CHANNEL AT:

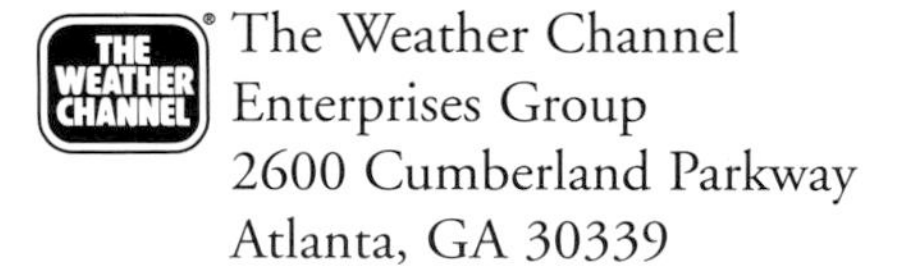

The Weather Channel
Enterprises Group
2600 Cumberland Parkway
Atlanta, GA 30339

or on the World Wide Web at:
http://www.weather.com

Other Products You Can Enjoy

STORM CHASER
WARREN FAIDLEY

You've read the book, now see the video! - Ride shotgun with Storm Chaser Warren Faidley as he pursues nature's untamed skies. A full hour of exciting video, including never before seen footage.
Storm Chaser Video. Product # 1056, Price: $19.95

Warren Faidley Posters - Warren Faidley, storm chaser, author and award winning photographer, captures the majesty of nature in these beautiful and stunning posters. Available separately or as a set, these full-color (17"x22") gallery quality prints are reproduced on heavy duty professional stock.
Supercell Storm - Tornado. Product # 1053, Price: $19.95
Wild Thing Lightning. Product # 1054, Price: $19.95
Set of Two Posters. Product # 1046, Price: $31.95

Everything Weather CD-ROM - The Essential Guide to the Whys and Wonders of Weather. A complete multimedia exploration of nature's forces, filled with fascinating information, footage and photographs of tornadoes, hurricanes, thunderstorms and more. It's all here, in this comprehensive reference from the most trusted name in weather - The Weather Channel.
Windows Version. Product # 1032-01, Price: $39.95
Macintosh Version. Product # 1032-02, Price: $39.95

SKY on FIRE Awe-inspiring and enlightening, this dynamic home video presents you with the high-voltage power and electrifying intensity of one of nature's most often viewed, yet underestimated forces - lightning! Experience the amazing qualities of these flashes of fire. 38 minutes.
Product # 1009, Price: $19.95.

TARGET-TORNADO An exciting home video! Join tornado chasers on their compelling quests and gain first-hand knowledge about the destructive, unexpected and sometimes unexplained behavior of these deadly, rampaging funnel storms. 45 minutes.
Product # 1005, Price: $19.95.

A collection of the most awesome and destructive storms from 1995. See nature's powerful forces in this exclusive tornado video chronicle, featuring rare, close-up footage, including six Texas twisters touch down simultaneously. 22 minutes.
Product # 1023, Price: $14.95.

No place on Earth has better weather.™

Order Form

It's easy to order:

- **Call Toll-Free 800-544-6206, Ext.: 18**
  (24 hours a day, 7 days a week)
- Fax your order to 313-416-8203
- Fill out the order form below and mail it to:
  BVE Products
  c/o The Weather Channel
  P.O. Box 2249
  Livonia, MI 48151-2249

☐ Mr. ☐ Mrs. ☐ Ms.

Name ______________________

Address ______________________

City ____________ State ____ Zip ________

Daytime Phone Number ______________________

Fax: ______________________

Payment Method: ☐ Check-(Payable to BVE Products, Inc.) ☐ Visa ☐ Mastercard

Credit Card # ______________________

Expiration Date ______________________

Signature ______________________

Allow 3-4 weeks delivery

Product Number	Description	Qty.	Price Per Unit	Total
			Merchandise Total	
			Shipping (See chart below)	
			2nd Day Rush Charge ($10.00)	
			Total Order	
			Sales Tax (GA & MI residents)	
			Total Amount Due	

Merchandise Total	Shipping Cost
Up to $23.90	$3.95
$23.91 - $49.95	$4.95
$49.96 - $69.95	$5.95
$69.96 +	$6.95